UNCORKED & OFF THE CHAIN

"In *Uncorked & Off the Chain*, Jameson Gregg shares with us his unique and funny take on all things. From ax handles to ticks to truth in advertising, Gregg's observations on the absurdity of modern-day life ring true. He says things you have thought, things that you wish you had said yourself. If you are looking for a politically correct, reverent tome, look elsewhere. If you are looking for an amusing read, this is the book for you."

—Raymond L. Atkins
Award-winning author of *South of the Etowah*

"Jameson Gregg is one of those rare comedic geniuses who sees the world sober as others see it after a few shots of bourbon, a Southern Jack Handey who can find humor in his own vasectomy and offer advice on preparing for mug shots. In *Uncorked & Off the Chain*, Gregg hones his lawyerly eyes on the absurdities of daily life, sending up his friends, his wife—not since the days of Mrs. Henny Youngman has a woman been beleaguered so—and himself. A fun, generous book that displays malice toward none, but mockery toward all, Gregg proves himself the rightful heir to Twain, Thurber, and lots of other very funny people. At a moment when the country could use some homespun good cheer, *Uncorked & Off the Chain* spins an insightful and hilarious web of wit."

—Jacob M. Appel
Award-winning author of *Einstein's Beach House*

"More than southern-engineered mansplaining, *Uncorked & Off the Chain* is chock-full of wry observational humor that made this Yankee broad laugh. From boozy jokes about bodily functions to adventures in dementia, reading this book will have you feeling like you're tipping a few with your pals in Grandma's basement. The more you drink, the funnier it gets."

—Linda Sands
Award-winning author of *3 Women Walk into a Bar* and *Grand Theft Cargo*

"Award-winning comic and author Jameson Gregg has blessed us once again with his hilarious *Uncorked & Off the Chain*, a collection of short monologues that could have come from any of the country's best comedy clubs. With a unique style—a mélange that echoes bits of George Carlin, Dave Chappelle, or a sophisticated version of Jeff Foxworthy—Gregg is at once funny and thought-provoking. It's a great read, and an inspiration for aspiring comics everywhere!"

—William Rawlings
Award-winning author of *Six Inches Deeper: The Disappearance of Hellen Hanks* and *The Girl with Kaleidoscope Eyes: A Novel*

"Like sitting down to a big ol' jar of mixed nuts: snips, scraps, odds, and ends from a brilliant if slightly skewed imagination, ranging from the goofily profound to the profoundly goofy. Reminiscent of Lewis Grizzard in one of his wackier moods."

—Man Martin
Award-winning author of *The Lemon Jell-O Syndrome* and *Paradise Dogs*

UNCORKED &
OFF THE CHAIN

UNCORKED & OFF THE CHAIN

Offbeat Ramblings of a Zany Comic

JAMESON GREGG

MOUNTAIN ARBOR
PRESS

Mountain Arbor
Press
Alpharetta, GA

ISBN: 978-1-63183-930-6 - Paperback
eISBN: 978-1-63183-931-3 - ePub
eISBN: 978-1-63183-932-0 - mobi

Printed in the United States of America   0 3 2 9 2 1

⊗This paper meets the requirements of ANSI/NISO Z39.48-1992 (Permanence of Paper)

"Fast Times in the Vomitory" originally appeared in slightly different form in *Modern Drunkard Magazine*, August 2005, under the pseudonym P. W. Lewis.

Cover by Maria Georgieva, a.k.a. Misha Design at 99 Designs

Author photo courtesy of Dominar Films, Athens, Georgia

Scripture quotations are taken from the Holy Bible, King James Version (Public Domain).

To my kid brother, Duffy, my most ardent fan until he departed this life much too soon.

*People who see life as anything more than
pure entertainment are missing the point.*
—George Carlin

*I have no taste for either poverty or honest labor,
so writing is the only recourse left for me.*
—Hunter S. Thompson

*An intelligent man is sometimes forced
to be drunk to spend time with his fools.*
—Ernest Hemingway

*The cracked ones
let the light in.*
—Unknown

Molly, Boss Dog

EMAIL VOODOO

Ever get emails with those annoying endings declaring, "If you don't forward this to five people in five minutes you will experience bad luck, chronic halitosis, and your pecker will fall off?" I immediately delete that rubbish.

My plan was working beautifully until last week when I deleted an email with a particularly ominous warning. I questioned my delete decision the second I made it but moved on.

Later that day, I suffered a flat tire and earned my first hemorrhoid trying to jack up the car with those flimsy, nail-file jacks they sell you these days. While grappling with a frozen lug nut, my wife called. My jack and I froze midair.

"I just collected the mail and a certified letter from the IRS is waiting for you at the post office."

Oh, shit. I dropped my forehead into my palms, sighed, and caught a whiff of my breath. *Oh, no. Halitosis!*

I finally attached the bicycle-tire spare and limped home quick as I could. Clutching my privates so they wouldn't fall off, I raced to open my email, retrieved the deleted culprit, and forwarded it to five people.

Life has been swell ever since.

MARS/VENUS NUTSHELL

Allow me to summarize the man/woman dynamic:
Men under-listen; women over-talk.

Of course, the reason men under-listen is *because* women over-talk.

And, of course, the reason women over-talk is *because* men under-listen.

It's the ancient circle of life.

LAUNDRY TIME

Your woman ever ask you to do the laundry? No doubt you had better things planned for that time slot.

Here's how you avoid this imposition: Next time, toss her favorite dress into the wash. Use the hottest water on the longest, roughest cycle. Then dry the living hell out of it.

Rehearse this line: "Hey, it somehow *accidentally* got mixed in. Can't blame me for an accident."

Bet she won't ask *you* to do the laundry again.

AUGMENTED REALITY

That's a hot phrase these days in the virtual world, where animation and video inject you right into the scene.

Guess what? The concept is ancient. Isn't that what pot smokers want to do—augment reality? Same for alcohol drinkers, pill takers, glue sniffers, needle junkies, and anyone who gets high.

I'm sure before battling a dinosaur, the cavemen chewed on special leaves and roots to augment reality, to make them strong and brave, to make them run faster and jump higher, to sharpen the aim of their spears.

So, to Silicon Valley millennials, don't come around claiming you invented "augmented reality." Your family tree is full of stoners.

OLE SPARKY

As a recovering lawyer, it's time to come clean. As required in step five of the AA twelve-step program, I hereby admit the exact nature of my wrongs.

I arrive early at our friends' Super Bowl party in hopes of stealing a moment alone with Ole Sparky, the gray-muzzled Humane Society–special mountain of a dog. I have a plan to enliven the party by teaming up with the hound.

Sparky and I are finally alone by the smoke-belching grill while our host hustles into the kitchen. Reaching into a deep pocket of my baggy pants, I remove a cleverly concealed ziplock bag laden with ground navy beans and peanut butter. My research revealed that duo to be the best alchemy for activating a dog's flatus factory, and Sparky laps it up as I knew he would.

Ten of us are lounging, drinking, and eating in front of the big screen with the pooch sprawled out in the middle of the scrum. I squint an eye to conduct clandestine recon.

At the kickoff starting the game's second half, the hound raises an ear to half-mast and his hind leg flinches. I alone know what's up. *Game on!* He twitches and spasms twice more, then Cooter suddenly blurts, "Oh my God, who farted?"

Suspicious glances dart across the room amid protests of innocence. Sparky flinches again. The stench grows undeniably obvious and Cooter yells, "Somethin's died in here!"

We hold our noses while fanning the air. Socrates points at the old dog and shouts, "You're the perp, you ole mutt!" Sparky stands, shimmies, and shakes. *What did I do?* Someone flings popcorn at the dog, pandemonium erupts, and a food fight is on.

Sparky is banished and order is restored. The game's score grows lopsided, a bust, but the canine is a hit—both real stinkers. Fortunately, no one lit a match.

Ole Sparky couldn't help it. The poor bastard loved the attention as much as he loved the navy beans and peanut butter.

Only the hound and I knew what really happened that night, and I knew he wouldn't tell. Now that he's passed, I reveal the truth in his honor.

CAMEL PEE

My wife is particular about furniture. Recently, I tragically spilled bourbon on one of our precious oriental carpets.

She jumped up from the sofa. "*Look what you did!* Quick, get towels and wipe it up. I'll grab stain remover before it sets."

"Relax, woman," I said. "I hear that over in Persia, they pour camel piss on newly woven rugs to break them in and to make them more valuable. Don't worry, I've only increased the value of that carpet. Poor me, on the other hand—I'll never recoup that bourbon."

TV TURF BATTLE

My wife and I are temporarily down to one TV. We're having some spats over who gets to watch what when. A comedy romance or UFC? Cooking show or college football?

I mention my dilemma to Socrates. He chuckles knowingly and offers his solution:

"When she's out of the room, set the channel where you want it, then take the batteries out of the remote. When she returns, tell her to change it back to *Pretty Woman*, or whatever. The remote won't work. You also try it to no avail, then curse the damn thing. She'll give up and head for the kitchen, where she ought to have been in the first place, and you can continue watching football in peace."

On sticky marital issues, Socrates knows his business.

#2 WASHTUB

The shrimp were running, so Cracker and I went cast-netting on my boat, an eighteen-and-a-half-foot outboard with a center console and built-in live bait well—a fishing machine sporting a great casting bow.

Cracker and I alternated between navigating the boat and casting the net. A successful cast is a beautiful thing — positioning the net and lines, planting the feet, torqueing the body, then snapping back all in one fluid motion while sailing the net so it unfurls and fully opens just before splashdown.

We were having moderate success snagging shrimp, fish, eels, the occasional shark, and those unidentified "Sailor's Choice" species that mysteriously lurk in these dark, southern, intracoastal waters. So as not to slime the deck, we dumped the flipping and squirming sea creatures into a round, galvanized-steel #2 washtub. (A #2 washtub, for the uninitiated, is about two feet in diameter, or for you philosophy majors, two feet across.)

We extracted "keepers" and tossed them into the iced cooler, dumped the dregs overboard, then cast anew.

Cracker was emptying the washtub overboard, offloading crabs and croakers, mud and mullet, when he said, "You know, the number-two washtub is epic in my family."

"Yeah," I said, "how's that?"

"My dad has been married and divorced five times. His philosophy is that it's time to move on when your wife's butt grows as broad as a number-two washtub."

Boom. Right there, my friends, is some good old-fashioned marital advice.

EGG SALAD

I recently hopped on a MARTA train, part of Atlanta's

public transit system. A portly woman with a nasty cold sat opposite, staring at me to beat the band, like *I* was the crazy one. She violently sneezed, and I swear half of an egg salad sandwich flew out of her nose.

Suspecting there would be more to this show, I shuffled to a faraway seat. Sorry to disappoint. We'll never know what happened next, but I'm sure that you, the learned and intuitive reader, will finish the story.

PUPPY LUV

✓ There's nothing more beautiful than a smoldering pile of puppy shit . . . that actually hit the wee pad.

✓ Once upon a time, while outdoors, I enjoyed the ambiance of nature—the breeze, sky, songbirds, trees. Now, all eyes must be on Molly, our Westie puppy. Can't miss witnessing a call from nature.

"Honey, did she go?" my wife always asks as Molly sprints through the door.

"No idea. I got lost in the blue sky and the snow-white clouds lazily floating past verdant treetops. They looked like giant cotton balls full of helium."

"My gosh," she'll reply. "That's lovely, but the two of you need to get back out there and don't come in until she goes."

✓ Theoretically speaking, if a puppy hurls and you discover it just as she is gobbling it back up, then she tosses it again, would that be like a twice-baked potato? How about refried beans?

✓ Used to be, while lounging on the throne to answer nature's call, I'd quietly read a book or magazine. Now, I multitask and play ball-toss with Molly.

✓ We finally trained her to conduct her business on a wee pad, but turns out, she's a poop walker. A whirlybird pooper.

Soon as the head of the first turd pokes out for a breath of fresh air, she starts wheeling 'round and 'round in the squatting position while drifting across the yard or room, all the while squeezing out cigarillos and jelly beans. Takes her about twenty serpentine feet to lay down a good dump. Walking 'round like a duck must help coax those babies out.

She begins an indoor BM on top of the wee pad with good intentions, but then who knows where they'll drop. I could lay out a twenty-foot landing strip, but she zigs and zags.

✓ Most of the time, life is peaches and cream around here, but as you can tell, sometimes it's cigarillos and jelly beans.

GOD'S GIFTS

God gave us bourbon, and life was good.

Then He gave us ice, and now life is really good.

BONELESS PORK

In a few years, all those young men who grew up with cell phones stored in their front trouser pockets next to their manhoods are going to start experiencing some serious erectile dysfunction.

Early studies are trickling in confirming that radiation emitted by cell phones kept beside the family jewels not only decreases fertility, but also increases the chances of serving up, *ahem*, boneless pork. It's a logical inevitability.

The limp-dick Gen Z and millennials who can't get it up with a crane won't be laughing at jokes about generic ED med names like mycoxafloppin and mydixabendin.

My advice: Invest in companies that make these pecker-picker-uppers. They'll be real growth stocks. Solid as a rock. Your cock may be a-floppin', but your IRA ain't gonna be a-droppin'.

SPEECHLESS

An eleventh-hour television interview with Roxie Brown after an F-3 tornado swept away her singlewide last night in Rattlesnake, Arkansas:

Interviewer: Miss Brown, can you tell us what happened?

Roxie: Oh my gosh. I'm speechless. I don't even know what to say. Words can't describe what happened. My baby and me run to my neighbor's trailer when I heard them sirens and we was lucky she let us in. I'm speechless. Her trailer has tornado straps. It shook something awful but didn't go nowhere. She lost her new outdoor patio set. It's gone. This is all my ex-husband's fault. I'm just speechless. I told him when my baby and me moved in after the divorce that he better put straps on our trailer. He ain't done it 'cause he never gets around to house chores. But fishin'? Oh my God. He always has time to fish. He sunk more money in that darn bass boat than we spent on our trailer. Words can't describe what I'm going through. It's like a cat got my tongue or somethin'. Part of the divorce was for him to pay the insurance on the trailer for two years. I don't know if he done it, but he better had or I'll take his ass back to court. And look at my Cadillac. A tree fell right acrost it and mashed it almost in two. I don't know what to say about that. I bought that with the money I got from the divorce. I can replace the trailer, but that Cadillac was a limited edition. I'm just speechless. Words can't describe it. I'm torn up. My heart's broken and I ain't even got no cigarettes. I hope my boss at the restaurant knows I won't be coming in today. All my work outfits was in that trailer and nobody can even tell me where it landed. My grandmother's crocheted quilt, my most prized possession after my Cadillac, is gone. I'm speechless about that too. I sure hope somebody finds it and returns it to me. I just don't know what to say. It's gonna take a long time for me to be able to talk about any of this.

VLADIMIR PUTIN

Did you know that some Slavic naming customs mirror those of some American Indian tribes?

Little-known facts about the birth of Russia's President Vladimir Putin and his naming rite recently came to light.

In the Vladimir tribe, the first name Vladimir is everyone's family moniker, and the last name is given. The given one is determined much like those with Indian handles such as Running Water and Hopping Rabbit.

Records reveal that the night before the birth of the future president, his father, Vladimir Pissin', ate a double order of the chef's special navy bean stew down at the Hammer & Sickle Café.

Upon the birth of the new Vladimir the next morning, in keeping with tradition, Mom held up their new baby and instructed Dad to walk outside and observe the first thing that came to his mind.

Timing was critical. Dad knew Mom detested flatulence, so he had held in his gas through the whole ordeal. Bloated like a drowned pig and on the verge of puking, he sprinted outside and proceeded to blow the trumpet for five solid minutes.

The newborn's name was obvious to Dad, but he knew Mom loathed terse, foul language, so "Vladimir Fartin'" wouldn't work. "What is our baby boy's name?" asked Mom as Dad sauntered through the door beaming relief.

"Vladimir Pootin', and he will rise to greatness." As so often happens in Russia, the clerk at the birth certificate bureau misspelled the name on the form, and that, my friends, is how Vladimir Putin got his name.

Now that these facts are public knowledge, I suggest our United Nations ambassador call Putin out on it, right there on the floor of the UN. "How can we take seriously a man named after an intestinal gust of wind?"

Putin's world influence will plunge. Russia won't bother us anymore.

Boom, problem solved.

(In the next installment of celebrity reveal, we learn that Colin Kaepernick's mother thought his father was a real asshole and Mom intended to get back at him in the naming of their child but didn't know how to spell "Colon.")

BUCK SNORTS

- ✓ A terrible mind is a good thing to waste.
- ✓ "Dysfunctional family" is redundant.
- ✓ As a rule, the fancier a man's car, the smaller his pecker. As for me, shucks, I'm okay driving a ten-year-old clunker.
- ✓ Any man who knows how to fold a fitted sheet is married or gay.
- ✓ Satellite radio stations are now broadcasting professional wrestling events. Did you get that—pro wrasslin' on the radio? I'm as big a fan as the next guy, but geez, one must be seriously eaten up with

it to listen to a match on the radio where the plot and ending are scripted and the only thrill is watching the showmanship.

✓ My tech guy is so good that he keeps changing his contact information without telling anybody in order to stay one step ahead of all those clients and would-be clients who beg for his time. He's that good.

✓ In OJ's defense, I think every Heisman Trophy winner should have one free pass at any felony of his choice. Well, okay, maybe two. Perhaps three.

FISHY 'ROUND THE GILLS

Some entries contained herein chronicle episodes of tipping the bottle while driving. Please don't think I am the only one ever to drive after a nip or two. According to the Centers for Disease Control, there are over three hundred thousand incidents of drinking and driving in the US every day. Luckily for us, the CDC estimates that the average drunk driver does so over eighty times before getting busted!

I am not condoning driving while drunk, or "fishy 'round the gills," as the British call it. Last time I stupidly did that was in my early twenties. Fortunately, no one was hurt. I've learned about designated drivers, taxis, rideshare companies, and crashing on friends' couches.

A problem with DUI laws is that one standard should not fit all. The blood alcohol test for DUI fails to consider the driver's tolerance level, experience, and ability. Are you an amateur or a pro? I can enjoy a pop or two and drive home just fine. Novices and bozos ruin it for the rest of us.

"Can you give me an example?" you ask.

"Easy." True story. Happened in 2004 in Marietta, Georgia. Two best friends in their twenties were drinking at a bar and became extremely shit-faced. On the drive home, the passenger was hanging his head out the window, probably hollering "RALPH!" while spewing his guts, when the driver veered off the road.

The truck sideswiped a telephone-pole support wire and decapitated the passenger! The snockered driver then drove twelve miles home and fell asleep in his bed, leaving his brainless best friend in the passenger seat.

A neighbor discovered the corpse in the parked truck the next morning and called the cops. They discovered the blood-drenched driver passed out and reeking of alcohol. Soon afterward, the police found the victim's head in the bushes near the telephone pole.

Research it if you think I'm spinning a tall tale.

That type of drunken behavior, my friends, gives drinking and driving a bad reputation. Gone is the Golden Era of Drunk Driving, when cops had a sense of humor about DUI.

Now the alcohol Nazis are trying to squelch the age-old tradition of the casual weekend drive in the countryside, a cold beer between your legs, taking in the ambiance, stopping occasionally to urinate on the road shoulder in front of God, the cows, and the farmer on his tractor on the far side of the pasture. No sir-ee, Bob, they'll lock you up for that these days.

There is an upside to dumb criminals swerving around our streets—the fools make the rest of us look good. Those of us who survive, that is.

Take the severed-head example. While cops were busy searching for the lost head, I'd just slide right on by in my car and tip my hat. As a gentleman who may have downed a few pints but with my faculties still intact, I would not have been their biggest concern at that moment.

Just remember, if you find yourself a bit tipsy and behind the wheel, don't lose your head.

GREAT NATION OR WHAT?

One fine evening, I innocently lounged in my man-cave recliner perusing the newspaper and firing off texts while watching the big screen, switching between football and baseball with dosh on each game. October, a beautiful time of year . . . college football *and* the MLB playoffs.

Google Assistant sponsored both games. Commentators asked questions such as, "Hey Google, what is the seating capacity of Wrigley Field?" The voice of the intelligent female assistant responded: "The seating capacity of Wrigley Field is forty-one thousand six hundred and forty-nine."

Commentators sprinkled questions to Google through-out the broadcast.

Q: Hey Google, what time is sunset in Los Angeles today?

A: Sunset in Los Angeles today is six eleven p.m.

Q: Hey Google, who holds the NFL record for most career touchdown passes?

A: Peyton Manning holds the NFL record for most touchdown passes. (Editor's note: Since surpassed by Drew Brees.)

The Google Assistant promos hooked me immediately. She easily answered any questions these sportscasters threw at her. That got me thinking about my own much-needed research. Why not feed the alcohol-infused ADD info-overload frenzy and acquire some useful information for you, the inquisitive, mature, adult reader?

I laid the newspaper aside, took up pad and pen, and teed up my smartphone.

Q: Hey Google, who has the biggest cock in the world? (Ed. note: This was a logical starting point of my research in that it relates to the deepest carnal desire of most men: a bigger man-root. As for Google, not all queries have easy answers. There is some dispute over who currently sports the biggest tally-whacker, hammer, love muscle, the largest johnson, willie, or one-eyed trouser snake. Seems like it's hard to distinguish facts from claims from myth from fantasy. Plus, they obviously do not have a database of all large pocket-rockets because mine was not in the online conversation. By the way, mine is so huge it still has snow on top in the summer.)

A: One lucky Mexican hombre named Cabrera may own the biggest yin-yang. He claims his is 18.9 inches, a real kidney-scraper, but there is suspicion that he is exaggerating. Imagine that.

Q: Hey Google, who has the biggest vagina in the world? (We don't discriminate here at Uncorked & Off the Chain.)

A: (Ed. note: Again, many claims are on the table.) The largest house of love may have belonged to the Scottish giantess Anna Swan, who sported a nineteen-inch happy valley. She stood seven foot eight, birthed a twenty-six-pound baby, and gave new meaning to "Grand Canyon."

Q: Hey Google, who is the most beautiful person in the world?

A: (Ed. note: The answer to that question apparently changes often according to the people who track these things.) As of this evening, that person is Deepika Padukone, the East Indian goddess and film actress.

Q: Hey Google, who is the biggest asshole in the world?

A: (Ed. note: Google Assistant is proper and detests foul language. She changed "asshole" to "a******," and refused to answer.)

Q: Hey Google, who is the biggest jerk in the world?

A: The biggest jerk in the world is a New Zealand man who, after contracting HIV, infected his sleeping wife with a tainted needle just so his misery could have company. Plus, he missed having sex with her.

Q: Hey Google, what is the world's largest turd?

A: The world's largest turd according to Guinness World Records is a fossilized dinosaur poop weighing over four pounds.

The claim for the longest human caca stands at twenty-six feet. Internet lore alleges that some guy ate a super fiber-rich diet and didn't defecate for a week due to a butt plug. At showtime, he proceeded to squeeze the cheese and laid down his magnum opus onto a bowling alley lane—a continuous twenty-six-footer, the entire length of his colon.

(Sorry folks, I gotta call bullshit on that one.)

Q: Hey Google, what is the best way to dispose of a dead body?

A: (Ed. note: Google actually answered this question, but oh my, now it's part of my permanent internet search records—twice now, because I had to return for fact-checking. One must be careful what one queries, but in this case, I took an arrow in the leg for you, the inquisitive reader.

I discovered multiple online articles using this very question as an example of what not to search because of the dubious imprint upon your cyberspace history. Now, with any missing body cases in my zip code, they will probably search my house with cadaver dogs and run me through a lie detector test.

Nonetheless, there is a disturbingly high number of learned online treatises offering assistance in the event one must clandestinely dispose of a human body. I will point out that many of these manifestos predated the deaths of Jeffrey Dahmer, John Wayne Gacy, and Ted Bundy. One wonders how many instructionals this trio penned using pseudonyms.

It's frightening what information is on the web these days. Many exposés are at your fingertips to educate on basic body-disposal facts, like proper disposition of teeth and DNA, those pesky telltale clues that can linger long after the deed. You can learn body destruction and/or disposal techniques ranging from burning, concrete boots in deep water, and dissolving in lye, to cannibalism, dumping into a landfill, and tossing into a pigsty.

Due to space constraints, I shall not dive into the weeds on any given technique, but as a public service, I've at least informed you that the information is available. If you really need to dig deeper, I recommend researching at a public library with a fake ID. If you get caught, please don't tell them I sent you.)

My football game ended in a lost wager, but the baseball game ran into extra innings thanks to my team's utter inability to hit a simple curve ball. Therefore, I was able to squeeze in a few bonus questions before bedtime:

- Most prolific prostitute: Sunny Lane, a fellow Georgian
- Largest feet: A Venezuelan man, sixteen inches long, size 26 shoe
- Longest ear hair: An Indian (dot, not feather) man, ten inches
- Best athlete ever: Martina Navratilova
- Longest orgasm: Rachel from Atlanta, who orgasms every thirty minutes (Afflicted with so-called "Persistent Genital Arousal Disorder," called a "disorder" by our muddling medical community. Nirvana is more fitting—Persistent Genital Arousal Nirvana.)

Imagine . . . enjoying such sports entertainment and having immediate answers to life's pressing questions, all from the comfort of your man-cave recliner. Is this a great nation, or what?

CHALK HER UP

I love "chalkin' women." Allow me to explain.

You see, I desire big ole heavy, plus-sized gals. (Don't ask me why.) Loved them way back since puberty. To me, it's a "natural" look, unlike the skin-and-bones toothpick look. I like my princesses plump. More cushion for the pushin', if you get my drift. I just love BBW — big, beautiful women. Rubbing their tummies brings me good luck and fortune. I guess you can call me a chubby chaser.

My woman's bigness must be well proportioned, that is, fat from the soles of her feet to the crown of her noggin and all points in between. I'm not interested in women who merely have excessive accumulations of fat on their buttocks, a.k.a. steatopygia (stē-ăt′ə-pĭj′ē-ə).

A man ought to hug all of his woman. With a chalkin' woman, you wrap your arms around her and she's so big, your hands can't touch around back. So, you chalk-mark where your prints left off. Then you shuffle around to her other side and hug her again, making sure you touch the chalk lines, and you've hugged all of her. That's my type of gal.

BBQ JOINT

Sensing that my cholesterol runneth low, I'm lunching alone today at a BBQ joint down the road. It shares a building with an Indian (dot, not feather) convenience store and a "no appointment necessary" beauty parlor.

Their pulled-pork sandwich is succulent. Like any authentic BBQ joint, there are a few black houseflies about.

I handle the sandwich with one hand while gently waving the other to keep the interlopers at bay. Two flies' hairy little legs skitter at lightning speed across the vinyl red-and-white-checkered tablecloth. Their trumpet-shaped proboscises sponge and vacuum food equally as fast.

Suddenly, they're fornicating right there across from my plastic basket, smack in front of God and my mustard greens!

Since the winged bastards can transmit dysentery, hookworms, and more, the knee-jerk reaction is to fan them away. Not me. My personal policy is never interrupt creatures when they are getting some action. Let the ole boy finish, then swat him, stomp him, or shoot him. But for heaven's sake, let him finish boinking.

I whip out my handy folding pocket magnifier and examine the ancient rite more closely. *Oh, my.* Do you know in which position flies make love? Doggy style, of course, like so many in the Wild Kingdom.

This ole boy is going to town and giving her the business at breakneck pace. The four thousand lenses in each of her wine-red eyes gyrate and roll in wild ecstasy, blurring like hypersonic kaleidoscopes.

A couple of the stud's hands grip and slap her buttocks. Another wraps around her black ponytail and yanks her head back. Two more massage her dangling, ample bosoms, tweaking her nipples as he rocks the bum dance, playing the *Musca domestica* version of hide the salami.

Wham, wham, wham.

When his two tiny vestigial wings start twitching like a dog's leg when you scratch his sweet spot, I figure the jig is up. Sure enough, just as suddenly as they started, he pulls out. They roll over and share a cigarette, apparently oblivious to my voyeurism. Then, *poof,* off to another table.

I'll return next week and try the brisket.

Pass the sauce, please.

VASECTOMY? JUST SAY NO

Contemplating a vasectomy, are you? Allow me to counsel against it. I am a victim of this barbaric medical procedure and sadly know the consequences firsthand.

A brief science primer: When a normal man ejaculates, about *two hundred million* sperm gush from his testicles, where they join forces with semen and surge like a tsunami down the "urethra" tube and through the penis where they spurt to glory.

It's meant to be a joyous occasion. Surfing sperm embark upon the only journey of their short lives, loyal soldiers carrying out their God-given duty to deliver a DNA package.

During a vasectomy, the doc slices through the scrotum then clamps the vas deferens tube just above each testicle through which sperm travel. In my case, he cinched those babies watertight.

As a result, my orgasms now go something like this: Two hundred million sperm resembling tadpoles sporting long, corkscrew flagellum tails take their starting positions on the blocks. Each hopes to win gold, to be the one and only one to squeeze through the membrane wall of the female egg.

The race director raises his starter pistol: "Swimmers, take your mark." A shot rings out as the announcer shouts, "They're off! Number 142,280,162 is out to an early lead, followed closely by numbers 8,641,029 and 62,194,032 . . ." He must enunciate each of the numbers, so calling these races requires the speed talk of an auctioneer.

Then something terrible and entirely unnatural happens—the racers slam their tiny heads against titanium clips and die on impact. Tails turned up, they slowly sink to their watery grave.

Meanwhile, as the next batch of horny competitors start mounting their blocks, two hundred million dead come floating down.

"That's not the way it's supposed to happen," the race director mumbles, but he's too busy to investigate since he must quickly register the two hundred million newcomers because nobody down there in the nutsack knows when the next clarion call may come.

Here's the scoop: This dramatic scene taking place inside my balls with every climax creates psychosomatic trauma for me. True, only one of the little swimmers per school could ever win the blue ribbon. The remaining 199,999,999 wrigglers are destined to perish anyway, but here's the tragedy: they don't take their *journey*. Life, my friends, is all about the journey. Peace out.

What is meant to be a grand and exciting event turns into brutal mass murder—the planned and systematic extermination of my entire future offspring.

Furthermore, I stand robbed of a nice income stream, a stud farm to be exact. Women would have paid exorbitant fees to line up in my living room awaiting their call to my bedchambers for a DNA shot.

My advice: Choose another form of birth control. Maybe just pull out early.

PARLEZ-VOUS FRANÇAIS?

It's good to throw around French words and phrases to show your sophistication, that you possess a certain level of *je ne sais quoi*. French is such a beautiful language, its words sounding grander than their English counterparts. Words flow off the tongue like silk fluttering in the wind.

For instance, my favorite soup is *soup du jour*. I love to say it and consume it. Problem is, restaurants can't seem to agree on exactly what it is. Some think it's cold potato soup, some think chicken noodle. It's all over the board. Don't you think culinary schools should reach agreement on a singular definition? All chefs put their own spin on recipes, but for Pete's sake, at least delineate the basic ingredients of *soup du jour*.

Why do *I* have to keep coming up with these suggestions? You'd think an educated populace would have figured this out by now.

In some cases, a French word doesn't translate very well on this side of the pond. Take *eau de toilette*. The product is lightly scented cologne, but the literal translation is "toilet water." No American wishes to splash toilet water behind their ears. (At least, let's hope not many.)

Before I knew the meaning, I was in the men's section of a department store and the salesclerk said, "May we interest you in *eau de toilette*?"

"Why are you asking me that?" I replied. "Do I *look* like I need to take a shit?"

Upon arriving home, I researched the word and

decided to try the product. I stopped in at another store and approached a salesclerk. "*Excusez-moi*, can you direct me to the *eau de toilette*?"

"Of course, honey. It's right over there under the sign that says 'Restroom.'"

FROMAGE BREATH

Why, at cocktail parties, do people serve food that creates bad breath? Folks stand around, drink in one hand, the other hand working the *hors d'oeuvre* table. As the evening progresses, everyone's breath transitions from cool mint to rotten egg. By the end, conversations are like boxers throwing punches.

A left cheese-stick jab.

An overhead garlic right.

A southpaw onion hook.

A right goat cheese uppercut.

Supercalifragilistic extra halitosis.

MISGUIDED MAXIMS

✓ "Low Man on the Totem Pole"

This expression connotes one at the bottom of the organizational chart. The wrongness of this one dawned on me one day when I was conducting totem pole research. In its construction, the lowest figure on the pole is generally the most respected.

Because totem poles are broader toward the base, the bottommost figure is typically the largest, most prominent, and adorned with the most detail.

If we are to keep "low man on the totem pole," it should henceforth refer to the CEO or chairman.

✓ "Nose to the Grindstone"

Really? Wouldn't that hurt? If you did it enough, it would wear your nose right off your face. You would have nothing but two holes where your nose used to be. A pig-nosed effect. Let's drop this one. We have enough ugly people running around.

✓ "I Could Care Less"

That means that you actually care to some degree. What you mean is, "I could not care less."

✓ "The Whole Kit and Caboodle"

What the hell is a caboodle? Is it possible to have half a kit and caboodle? Can you have the whole caboodle without the kit? (Turns out you can have a caboodle without the kit, and they're available at Walmart.)

✓ "You Don't Say!"

Maybe the dumbest expression ever. Of course she said it or you wouldn't be saying, "You don't say!"

✓ "Today Is the First Day of the Rest of Your Life"

Really? What about tomorrow? Maybe yesterday was the first day of the rest of your life. Who knows? The more valuable information would be knowing if today is the last day of your life. Then you could get your affairs in order. Destroy all those secret, hidden items you don't want your spouse/children/ executor to find: porn, drugs, gambling records, communications with your secret lover, and so on. Data is mysteriously stored everywhere in the bowels of your computer, so remove the hard drive and toss it into the lake. If you don't know how to remove the hard drive, throw the whole damn computer in the lake.

✓ "Top of the Day"

It's disingenuous for you to flippantly say "top of the day" to someone before the day is complete.

"Wow. I almost said 'top of the day' to Becky when I met her for lunch at that new Italian restaurant. Glad I didn't say it, because actually, the top came later when my Keno numbers hit and I won a hundred dollars on a one-dollar ticket."

The only way to know what the top of your day was is through reflection as you sip that nightcap with your feet propped up. We need to be more precise with our language.

✓ "There's More Than One Way to Skin a Cat"

Really? Does PETA know about this? What kind of sick SOB made this discovery, anyway?

PULL MY FINGER

Okay, you've got me dead to rights—some flatulence and scatological humor snuck their way into this book. But

I'm not the first (and won't be the last) to utilize this form of comedy. Aristophanes, the Father of Comedy, employed many a fart joke in his fifty-century BC plays, and this fine art marched forward through time, evolving into the likes of Larry the Cable Guy, who ate too many hot dogs in the parking lot of a building-supply super store and pooped in the display toilet. Jay Leno was speechless but the audience roared.

Some literary agents would never represent a purveyor of scatological humor. As a result, they would reject, in addition to Aristophanes and Larry the Cable Guy, Geoffrey Chaucer (from *The Canterbury Tales*, "The Miller's Tale" and "The Summoner's Tale"), William Shakespeare (*King Lear*, *The Comedy of Errors*, *Othello*, *Two Gentlemen from Verona*, *Henry IV*), Benjamin Franklin ("A Letter to a Royal Academy"), Mark Twain (*1601*), and J. D. Salinger (*The Catcher in the Rye*), among many others.

Flatulence humor is probably as old as humankind. *Homo erectus* and their ancestors likely enjoyed it as a main source of entertainment. With their diet of raw meat, roots, and berries, surely there were copious amounts of intestinal backfires, honks, and buck snorts. Once they discovered fire, they probably burned down many a woods with pyro-flatulence, the art of lighting one's fart, otherwise known as a "blue angel."

The whoopee cushion dates to the third century AD, for Pete's sake, when Roman Emperor Elagabalus planted "air pillows" in the seats of dinner guests, especially the more pompous invitees.

Admittedly, scatological humor is the most simplistic and base form of humor, the lowest-hanging comic fruit of them all. (And thus, my editor/wife, in her disgust, said, "We grew up in different circles." "No," I replied, "different locker rooms.")

While many maintain some semblance of their childhood humor as they age, it's the youngsters who are most tickled by a well-timed fart. Adults drill into children the cultural taboo of discussing such issues and kids delight in defying those taboos. So, yes, by weaving in a few narratives on the topic, whether they be real or imagined, I'll take credit for this public service, for enticing younger generations to enjoy reading and to appreciate books.

Enough with this intro and the apologies. Excuse me, please, nature calls. I must go birth a Yankee.

TRICK ON BASEBALL

If you have the spare time and the years to set it up, pull this trick on the game of baseball.

Attend all the clinics, do all the homework, whatever necessary to become an umpire. The higher you go, the longer it'll take, from T-ball to major league baseball.

Let's say you make it to the high school level. There's a big rivalry game and you are the home plate umpire calling balls and strikes.

Here's what you do: call every pitch a strike. In the dirt: *STEE—RIKE.* Over the batter's head: *STEE—RIKE.* Hit the batter: *STEE—RIKE.* Doesn't matter. *STEE—RIKE.*

How long will it take before they give you the hook? Ever seen an umpire get ejected midgame? Me neither. Chances are that amped-up dads will leap from the stands and whip your ass before anything official happens.

CRIME BEAT

The following are from my local newspaper's crime beat with my commentary added:

- ✓ "A woman said she loaned her mom $60 and she won't pay her back."

   Holy mackerel, she called the cops! Wonder in which socioeconomic strata these folks live.
- ✓ "A man was arrested at the county courthouse after he showed up intoxicated for a DUI hearing."

   I like this guy's style.
- ✓ "A seventy-nine-year-old man was arrested at Walmart and charged with assault."

   Yeah, baby, you go. At seventy-nine, the old boy still has some spunk. Next time, don't stop at assault; go for battery as well. You're never too old to beat the shit outta somebody. Might as well throw in obstruction of justice, terroristic threats, and resisting arrest. Need to juice up those crime reports.
- ✓ "A man was arrested for driving a riding lawnmower on the highway while intoxicated."

The poor guy was probably just trying to get to the store to buy more beer. Under these circumstances, you need to help a brother, not arrest him.

CALL FROM BEYOND

Traveling the interstate, true story, a splashy lawyer billboard drew my attention:

"KILLED OR INJURED? Call [phone number]"

Really? He's seeking calls from the dead. How does that work? Is there cell reception in heaven and hell? By séance?

Anyway, I wrote down the guy's number and stuck it in my wallet. If I suffer a wrongful death, I may ring him up when I arrive in heaven.

CASANOVA

Cooter, one of my golf trip buddies, is loud, funny, and off the chain. When he looks in the mirror, he doesn't see graying hair, glasses, and a potbelly. He sees Brad Pitt.

In the evenings after golf, he loves to guzzle a few scotches while we dine, then show off with the ladies in front of his mates. One evening, there was a table of younger, good-looking babes across the way.

"Hey, Roberto." Cooter motions to our waiter. "Come over here for a minute."

Roberto hustles over.

"See those girls at that table?" Cooter says with a wink

as he's slipping him a twenty. "Go over and tell them I'm a TV star and ask them to guess which show."

It is one of Cooter's standard icebreakers. We observe Roberto chatting up the ladies. They turn their heads our way.

"What do you reckon they'll guess?" Cooter says. "A soap opera star? A game show host? Reality show?"

Roberto returns with a smirk.

"And what did they guess?" Cooter asks.

"Antiques Roadshow!"

Cooter was uncharacteristically sedate for the balance of the evening.

SWIMSUIT ISSUE

As a longtime *Sports Illustrated* subscriber, I grow excited as the annual Swimsuit Issue nears. Gotta keep up with clothing styles, right? My wife stays in touch with fashion, too, yet she poo-poos the Swimsuit Issue. It is for this reason, when the Issue is due, I try to beat her to the mailbox, to spare her the grief. This year I failed.

She stormed into the house, plopped the magazine in front of me, and delivered her usual lecture. It was even worse this year because she had just heard the latest scuttlebutt in the beauty salon about SI models.

"You men are sick," she scolded. (I think she truly believes it too.) "You ogle over photoshopped pictures of starving twelve-year-old children."

Later that night, after a few cocktails, I felt brave and

emboldened, so I revisited the topic with her. I was thinking with great clarity. My tongue was well oiled and I spoke in a very eloquent fashion. I explained why it's perfectly okay for grown men to study pictures of "teenage" girls in swimsuits.

I felt victorious as we laid our heads on our pillows. My speech nailed it, confirmed the next morning over breakfast.

She said, "I'm glad we had that talk last night about the Swimsuit Issue. I understand now. I never thought of it that way before."

So it worked! Whatever I said worked.

Problem is, fellows, I was awash with drink when I uncorked my soliloquy and can't recall what I said.

Sorry, guys. I was *t-h-i-s close* to delivering a golden drop of man wisdom but lost it in the ether. If I ever recall it, I'll tweet it out.

FLEX SEAL

Ever seen those TV commercials for Flex Seal? Phil Swift, the Flex Seal cofounder and pitchman, performs all manner of seemingly impossible feats with the almighty power of Flex Seal and related family of products that can solve just about any problem. It must be all the rage, judging by the ever-increasing frequency of the commercials. Flex Seal appears to be on pace to acquire Google and Apple.

Flex Seal Phil, product salesman extraordinaire, is extremely happy and motivated. His latest stunt is cutting a giant hole in the bottom of a boat and repairing it with only Flex Tape Clear. He blissfully zooms across open waters then slows as a frenzy of sharks circle and lurk under the boat. Oh, what a man!

I finally succumbed and purchased a roll of Flex Tape that I secretly keep by my bedside for the sole reason that my wife may one night follow through on her threats to cut me "wide and even." I figure with the tape, I can patch the chasm in the flesh until the ambulance arrives.

Thanks, Phil.

A PITY

While grocery shopping the other day, the most gorgeous woman ever appeared ahead walking toward me down the aisle. I did a double-take before diverting my eyes and straightening my posture.

She stopped to examine salad-dressing selections. I stopped to clandestinely examine her—a rare sight, feminine beauty in its purest form. I admired her raven-black hair, olive skin, and coral outfit as she gracefully reached for a bottle of dressing, glanced at the label, and placed it in her buggy.

She moved closer. In an enchanted, adrenaline-infused stupor, I nudged my glasses higher on the bridge of my nose, hiked up my pants, ran my fingers through my hair, licked my lips, extended my jaw to eliminate my double chin, and cleared my throat.

Our eyes locked for an instant. *Eye contact*, can you

believe it! Hers were a stunning, deep, ultramarine blue into which a man could tumble head over heels and never stop.

Then, in a voice dripping with seduction and spoken through perfect lips, she said, "Hi. How are you doing?"

I smiled and stammered, "Just . . . just fine. How are *you* doing?"

"Yes," she spoke *into her earbud*, which I hadn't noticed before, "but some old pervert is hitting on me."

Sometimes life is a pity, ain't it?

OPEN BAR

We were at the funeral of an old friend who was quite the connoisseur of adult beverages, a real elbow bender. He was a "heavy drinker" in my estimation, and not an alcoholic, because he balanced his prolific consumption with a long and successful career as an engineer. His obituary (I'm not making this up) listed thirteen things he loved most. Among them:

- Family—eleventh
- Beer—fourth
- Bourbon—first

Socrates leaned over during the service and whispered, "If the preacher were to announce an open-bar reception, that coffin lid would fly open."

HELLO, DRONE

These days, when I spot a suspicious low, slow-flying airplane or drone, I find an open spot among the trees, stand tall and proud, thrust my fist high, and shoot the bird.

It's probably a flyby updating the goings-on at my house to sell to the highest bidder in the entire universe—without my permission and against my will. It could be a private company, or it could be any one of the government alphabet soup agencies keeping an eye on us *for our own protection*.

If they have the right to invade my privacy and photograph me in my backyard, I have the right to shoot them a bird, don't you think?

URINATION EDIFICATION

The National Institute of Restroom Hygiene and Behavior just released the results of a nationwide three-year study. They planted hidden cameras and microphones in men's restrooms in large office buildings across the land, concentrating only on urinals and washbasins. After secretly observing the habits of over one hundred thousand urinators, this is what they concluded:

When someone is standing beside them at the urinal, men fart only 8 percent of the time and wash their hands 97 percent of the time. But when alone, they fart a whopping 91 percent of the time and wash their hands a paltry 12 percent of the time.

The Institute was quick to point out that their data does not include silent farts.

BEAUTY

The triangle formed by our eyes, nose, and mouth is mostly what determines "beauty." Studies, academic and otherwise, abound on the phenomenon.

My observations reveal that about 10 percent of people are truly beautiful, 10 percent truly ugly, and the rest of us fall somewhere in between.

Except when you feel needy and amorous. Then the percentage of beautiful people rises proportionately to the burn level in your loins.

The percentage invariably skyrockets at a bar's closing time. In a few instances, I've witnessed it rocket up to 100 percent in some guys' minds, where ALL THE LADIES are beautiful, a place you don't want to go. Trust me on that.

THE FLYING CLOUD

At seventeen years old, I owned a driver's license and a piece o' shit for a car. I "needed" to drive to a Pink Floyd concert with some friends, so Mom graciously let me borrow "the Flying Cloud"—her prized possession, a rode-hard but spacious Buick. She was a 1967 sky-blue, four-door hardtop Electra with fins running down the hind ridges flanking the trunk.

The Flying Cloud derived her name from her fins and

her color, but little did Mom know it also often described my occasional state of sobriety when I was her pilot.

The afternoon of the big road trip, Mom cleaned that land yacht from stem to stern so the Flying Cloud would sparkle for my friends. Even got on her hands and knees and shampooed the floorboard carpets. Bless her heart.

Beer flowed in abundance on the two-hour trip highlighted by an emergency, broad-daylight piss stop on the shoulder of I-95. We were all underaged drinkers, but luckily, we had a professional driver — *moi.*

Timmy guzzled like a greenhorn, still learning to gauge how much is too much. We each snuck a whiskey flask into the coliseum. During the concert (which was beyond awesome, btw), I lost track of the number of corn dogs Timmy scarfed between slugs from his flask.

On the drive home, all hell broke loose as the bastard jettisoned barf for the ages. Oh, he didn't just spit up a little; he blew a whole bag of groceries. He cried "RALPH!" like a bull moose in rut. He yorked a river and flooded the Flying Cloud's immaculate carpet. *Vomitus maximus.*

Timmy's fellow backseat passenger royally cussed him out as he contorted to avoid splatter. Collateral damage to him was the least of my worries as I struggled amid the chaos to keep the Flying Cloud between the lines and out of the ditch.

I couldn't pull onto the road shoulder for fear of getting busted while that son of a bitch couldn't even muster the courtesy to crank his window down and hang his head out — telephone support wires notwithstanding. I soldiered on with all windows down as the stench swirled through the car, prompting dry heaves even in me, the consummate professional.

After delivering my passengers, I arrived home and cut the lights as I eased the Flying Cloud into the driveway. I tried wiping up puke until I felt fishy 'round the gills myself. All I could manage was swirling it around with newspaper before shooting stars and vertigo overcame me. I snuck into the house and passed out stone cold and fully clothed.

Crack of dawn, I awoke with a headache from hell and to Mom hollering in the driveway as she surveyed the Flying Cloud parked cattywampus in the driveway. Her cries must have carried clear over to the next county.

After that excursion, and for some reason, sadly my parents never again allowed me to borrow their cars for rock concerts. Sometimes parents just have no sense of humor.

BUCK SNORTS

- ✓ MLB Gamblers Quiz: What's the scariest thing about betting on the visitors? Bottom of the ninth.
- ✓ True storefront sign: "We treat you like family." No sir, I'm not shopping in there.
- ✓ Do the math on the cost of maintaining your teeth for life—flossings, cleanings, fillings, mending cracked and chipped ones, caps, bridges, root canals, etc.—vs.

one-time dentures. Financial planners ought to rec-ommend yanking the teeth and going straight to den-tures at the earliest age possible.

✓ Just for fun, while ordering in the fast-food drive-thru, insist that the order is TO GO. See what they say.

✓ Plastic surgeon sign: If life gives you lemons, simple surgery can give you melons.

✓ As a sports gambler, you know you're in trouble with thirty seconds left in the football game and you need a pick-six followed by an onside kickoff recovery followed by a successful Hail Mary. Go ahead and turn the lights out.

AL CAPONE, AMATEUR CRIMINAL

Public intoxication is a misdemeanor. In my state of Georgia, the penalty is up to $1,000 and/or up to one year in jail.

That said, I've downed my share in bars. Since passing the Georgia Bar, I've not passed up many more. Is a bar a "public place"? It is in some states. The police can bust you for intoxication even inside a watering hole. In any event, when you step out onto the sidewalk, you are surely in public.

If popped for public lubrication each time, my rap sheet would make Al Capone look like a rank amateur.

NO-HANKIE ZONE

When I was a kid, my parents invited an elderly couple over for an "important dinner."

"You better behave yourself, you hear?" Mom warned. So I ate and observed mostly in silence.

During the feast, the VIP gentleman pulled a white handkerchief from his back pocket, covered his nose, and . . . *HONK, HONK.*

He held out the hankie and examined the results, squinting his eyes and tilting his head like a dog hearing a high-pitched sound. He c-a-r-e-f-u-l-l-y folded it, folded it again, reinserted it into his back pocket, and carried on as if nothing just happened.

Oh my gosh, I wanted to scream, *DID YOU SEE THAT!* I glanced at Mom and she fired a clandestine and stern no across my bow. I dared not peek at my brother.

I could not stomach any more dinner, for I kept thinking of that full, wet, sticky hankie squishing around in his pocket. Probably leaking through and staining my parents' chair.

At a young age, I thus realized that we Americans are too loose with our behavior at mealtime.

The hankie blow at the dinner table may have been acceptable back in the day, but please, can we end this tradition? Can't we excuse ourselves from the dinner table and slip off to the restroom to handle this bodily excretion in private?

Flash to the present. We need updated, common sense,

enlightened legislation focusing especially on mealtime commercials.

I like to catch a spot of TV news while lunching. Apparently, watching TV in the middle of a weekday unwittingly slots one into a certain demographic: elderly, ailing, and in need of a POCKET CATHETER.

That's right, I'm minding my own business, trying to finish leftovers, when husband and wife appear on screen strolling outdoors, a very happy couple because they use Jack & Jill pocket catheters. How romantic.

And how appetizing. I'm hoping to finish my peas and carrots in peace and suddenly I'm forced to think about shoving a sixteen-inch tube up my own rod until I hit pay dirt inside my bladder, all just to get a little piss action.

(Note to medical providers: When my time comes, I will need a custom catheter. A sixteen-inch tube simply will not reach my bladder, since it must first traverse an eighteen-inch telephone pole.)

The pocket catheter advertiser offered free samples. Hey, there's an idea. Take a test run next time during lunch. Run the tube up your willie with one hand while the other hand shovels food into your pie hole, all the while watching their commercial. The circle of life remains unbroken.

Another example: Tonight, I was watching the news and eating enchiladas, and *BAM*, a blaring advert for colorectal cream. I will spare you the details of the dreaded rectal itch—the symptoms, how to apply the product, and the rest—in case you are eating while reading this. They sure didn't extend me that courtesy while I was eating.

It's time to outlaw mealtime commercials that invoke gross bodily functions or ailments. The list should include, *but not be limited to*, catheters, colostomy bags, enemas, tampons, laxatives, hemorrhoid cream, and any product used to treat toe fungus, warts, ear wax, anal, penile, or vaginal leakage, smegma, dandruff, bad breath, toe cheese, open sores, hammertoe, eyelash mites, boogers, farts, psoriasis, ringworm, dingleberries, elephantiasis, flesh-eating disease, gingivitis, skin shedding, liver disease, herpes, halitosis, pinworms, or tapeworms!

ULTIMATE COLON CLEANSE

Ever shop at those vitamin stores and fall prey to a sales clerk pitch on the benefits of a colon cleanse? First, they try convincing you that you have a serious predicament. Then, of course, they have the perfect remedy.

It's happened twice to me now, same store, same overweight guy. "I cleanse every week," he enthusiastically proclaimed, "and I've never felt better in my life."

I didn't stop in to analyze (anal-yze) the contents of his colon or mine. I just wanted some fucking vitamin C. Chapped my ass. Did I *look like* I needed a colon cleanse?

Pissed, I wished a pox upon him, an old-fashioned, medieval disembowelment, *Braveheart* style—the ultimate colon cleanse.

"How's that for a colon cleanse, my friend?"

LATINO BEAT

Today I pulled up beside a car full of Latinos at a stoplight. Their windows were open and music blared and, *OMG*, it was the same tune they play in Mexican restaurants. They actually listen to it in their spare time! Hey, I'm down with it. *Viva la música española.*

BURP

A terrible habit I have developed, one that I recommend to you.

When I expel gas noisily from my stomach through my mouth, a.k.a. burp, I enunciate the word aloud. It's immensely satisfying to actually say b-u-r-p with the very lips over which the act is occurring *and* have the sound of the word match that of the act so perfectly.

Please carefully reread the previous sentence. This amazing convergence of audible factors has no equal.

Linguists through the ages have sought phonetic accuracy when spelling sounds. "Imitative spelling" is what they call it, and some hit the mark better than others. Some are used to describe a wide variety of sounds. Take "crunch," for instance.

"Crunch," an oft-used imitative spelling, can describe a

kid eating cereal, a fender bender, an arthritic knee bending back and forth, biting into a crisp apple, and walking on dry leaves. "Crunch" phonetically describes them all, which makes "crunch" an imitative whore.

Not the case with "burp." It is singular in its use. Oh, sure, you could say, "My car's muffler burped loudly," but that explosion from the tailpipe doesn't sound like a real burp, which the dictionary says emanates from the stomach. Poetic metaphors like the car muffler example don't count.

The first known use of the word "burp" was in 1929. Whoever first spelled it nailed it. Would its translation into other languages also be imitative? No. The Spanish translation is *eructo*. Try saying that next time you burp. Doesn't work. How about the Polish translation: *beknięcie*? Or the Arabic translation: تجشؤ ?

So, try it next time a burp is brewing. It feels good. Practice in private at first. Experiment with voice inflection—tone, pitch, volume.

Then, when you have the right audience, debut your new skill. The greatest shock value will be that first time, so choose wisely. Maybe at Thanksgiving dinner. Gotta make it a loud one. Watch Grandma jerk back in horror and cough her dentures into her mashed potatoes as you unveil your latest stroke of genius in what will surely be one of your finest hours.

Granted, from a spiritual perspective, enunciating a burp is not as fulfilling as letting fly a fart, but it's close. I predict a grassroots movement, a phenomenon that spreads like a virus, and in no time, it will be common practice at pubs, in school cafeterias, and around camp-fires all across the land.

SAY WHAT?

CARPET BOMBING

You'll occasionally hear of a military operation called "carpet bombing." Sounds like a humanitarian thing to do. I guess the recipients live on dirt floors. Wish they'd drop some around here. We have a couple of rooms in need of new flooring. Taupe would be nice.

As I analyze more deeply, why discriminate against wood, tile, slate, laminate, and linoleum flooring in favor of carpet? We should encourage diversity. I realize that carpet would have practically no breakage on impact, but if properly crated and parachuted, you could drop hard-wood-floor bombs virtually anywhere.

SECTARIAN VIOLENCE

World news frequently reports on what they call "sectarian violence," especially in the Middle East. I'm no foreign policy wonk, mind you, but I have a solution.

Employers in the Middle East must first understand that secretaries are people who like appreciation and fair treat-ment. So, give 'em some flowers now and then. Give 'em a raise. Create a National Sectarian Day like we have in the US. You don't hear about that much sectarian violence over here.

CANCER WARNING

With all the money we spend on cancer research, why is it left to me and my one-man laboratory to identify, in groundbreaking fashion, a very important cancer-causing agent?

It dawned on me recently as I was eating soup. (Sidebar: Does one eat soup, or drink it? Consuming soup is uncommon for me because as long as I have teeth, I prefer to grind, pulverize, chomp, and masticate my meals—preferably meat. One doesn't "eat" something one can suck through a straw. One doesn't eat a milkshake, one drinks it. Likewise, one doesn't eat soup, one drinks it, even if administered one spoonful at a time.)

Back to cancer. It hit me recently as I was drinking soup—some red-colored soup from a box. I nuked a bowl in the microwave and, as I sat to drink it, read the ingredients printed on the package. Turns out, it was "tomato basil soup."

When the lightbulb flashed, I jumped up and spit a mouthful into the sink then gargled with mouthwash. I remembered that a good friend recently contracted basil cell carcinoma. *Boom*, there you go. Eat the basil soup, get the basil cancer.

It's purely brilliant of me to make the connection. Alfred Einstein pointed out that it's genius when one pairs two concepts in a way never done before.

Let the medical research nerds run with that one. I'd conduct my own studies but I'm a high-concept man. It would be a colossal waste for me to get into the weeds on a single issue, important though it may be. That's why God gave us lab rats and lab geeks.

LAISSEZ-FAIRE CAPITALISM

How can the central theme of any capitalistic economic system be rooted in laziness? It won't work; I don't care how fair it is or how you spell it.

AT THE RESTAURANT

Diner to waiter: Do you have a good béarnaise?

Waiter: I'll be delighted to ask our sommelier. [Waiter returns moments later.] Sorry, sir, no béarnaise, but we have a nice Beaujolais.

Diner: How about beurre blanc?

Waiter: I will be happy to check, sir. [Waiter departs/returns] It appears we have no beurre blanc, but we do offer a splendid blanc de blanc as well as a full-bodied Fumé Blanc.

Diner: I see. Do you have prosciutto?

Waiter: [Departs/returns] So sorry again, sir. No prosciutto, but we offer a very popular Prosecco.

Diner: Well, well, well, do you even have vichyssoise?

Waiter: [Departs/returns] We are sold out, but I'm happy to offer a light-bodied, crisp verdicchio.

Diner: That's okay, I'll just take the chicken.

DOCTORS

I swear, I don't know what it is about doctors. There

must be a shortage. Goes for their staff too. It's always wait, wait, then wait some more.

My doctor is with one of those mega-practices with dozens of practitioners. The other day I called his office to schedule an appointment. They put me on hold f-o-r-e-v-e-r. Sales pitches for various departments scrolled repeatedly, offering solutions for almost every ailment, existing and imagined.

Every two minutes, a recorded male voice broke in: "If you have a medical emergency, please hang up and call 911 immediately." I started recording the number of times I heard the 911 advice, using the tally system—four strokes down then a slash to make five.

As I tallied the first bundle of five, I began wondering how long this could continue. *How high can my blood pressure rise before my head explodes?* Toward the end of the second bundle, it dawned on me that I didn't initially have a medical emergency, but I was quickly developing one!

There he goes again—*eleven.* I may find the guy whose voice is on the recording and strangle him.

Two more minutes of adverts and here he comes again—*twelve.* I'm going to cut his tongue out.

We're heading toward not only a medical emergency, but a criminal one too. I envision having a heart attack at the same instant the police are carting me off for murder.

One more time and I'll rip his head off, spit in his neck, then—suddenly, a live person comes on the line. "So sorry you had to wait. How may I help you?"

I longed to tell her to shove it up her sweet ass and that

I'm moving my business. *Ha, ha.* Not on a bet. Go through all that new patient registration crap all over again? No sir. Suck it up and go.

"Yes, good morning," I replied through a gritted-teeth smile. "I'm calling to schedule an appointment, please, blah, blah, blah."

Am I a big pussycat, or what?

When the appointed time approaches, they bombard me with multiple robocall reminders, and never at a convenient time. Usually during naptime, mealtime, or during sporting events with a bet hanging in the balance and live-action possibilities.

Their calls, texts, and emails encourage me to arrive fifteen minutes in advance (so I can get a jump on the one-hour wait!).

Other than the aggravation, I suspect it's actually good to have to wait for your physician. That means he/she is probably good. Who would tolerate a load of hassle for a *bad* doctor? It's probably a sign of a quack or a newbie if you can walk right in.

Small consolation: The best magazine articles are ripe for stealing from medical waiting rooms. I don't buy magazines that teach me, for example, "How to Make a Woman Climax Just by Looking at Her," or "How to Make a Million Dollars This Month while Lounging in Your Underdrawers on the Couch."

There is an art to the clandestine removal of magazine pages, folding then slipping them into your pocket so your fellow patients-in-overdue-waiting don't notice.

It's gratifying to steal from doctors. It's social justice. They expect it, so don't disappoint.

A DOG'S LIFE

When Molly is instructed to hop into the car, she doesn't know if she's destined for a ten-minute or a ten-day trip. Must be tough, not knowing how to pack your bags.

Bones! Yes, we'll need bones! Grab a sack of those nubby chicken ones! And snacks, we'll need those! How about a couple of boxes of bacon-flavored biscuits! Let's not forget treats, yesyesyes, treats! Those little square ones that taste like cows are my favorite! Sticks! Oh boy, oh boy. We better go outside and find a couple of good sticks to take along! Tennis balls too! I'm ready. What are we waiting for?

GIRL GONE BONKERS

Calamity struck my balance sheet recently when Costco opened one of its retail-orgy warehouses just down the road. Now, every day is Christmas for my wife. She knows she can hop in her car anytime and soon be in warehouse club heaven. Costco sells quality merchandise, but only in bulk. No bags at checkout, only boxes. It's a food paradise for NFL linemen, Sasquatches, and other giants. Don't go there thinking small ball.

CONSUMERISM ON STEROIDS

She has created a storage nightmare at our house. For

each one thing we have aplenty, there is no longer room for twenty other things. We have enough kale and chia chips to last 'til end times, but we've no room for salt, pepper, or ketchup. We have 250 cans of baked beans, one hundred bottles of laundry detergent, fifty packs of frozen chicken, a partridge in a pear tree, and enough toilet paper to service Sherman's army, but sadly no room for fruits, nuts, or beer. She's got the fever, I tell you.

CONSUMERISM GONE MAD

Our freezer and fridge are chock-a-block. Lose electricity and I'm out a month's wages. She can't seem to grasp the point that Costco is going to be there tomorrow and the next day. If it goes away, something else will take its place. No need to hoard.

"I've got to go back soon so we can save some more money," she announced today.

"Honey, I don't think we can afford to save any more money this month."

I envision my plea to the bankruptcy judge: "Your Honor, yes, we burned through all our money and there's none left for creditors, but look how much we saved!"

DREADED RETAIL FEVER

What's a poor fellow to do? I know about Compulsive Buying Disorder and have flashbacks of my friend's vast basement stacked wall to wall with shopping bags, price tags still intact on clothes he'll never wear. Next thing you know, my wife will buy a storage shed for backup. This is not survivalism, not commercialism, but consumerism schizo-style.

She claims her "condition" is not as bad as I let on, but it's a matter of perception, right?

Somehow, I must snap her out of this serial shopping. I'm thinking bypass the group therapy stage and go right to good ole-fashioned electroshock therapy.

SPORTS COMMENTATORS

Ever watch golf on TV? It slays me when a golfer hits it close to the hole and the commentator says something like, "Golly, he could not have hit it any better," or, "She hit a perfect shot."

Bullshit. If the ball doesn't go in the hole, it isn't the perfect shot. These folks shouldn't be so loose with our language.

Similar hyperbole among NBA commentators. In that league, if a guard drives the basket, the best athletes in the world will defend him. His defender will ride his flank as he contorts to sneak his shot under the wingspan of a crashing seven-footer. He'll miss and the commentator will say, "Oh, he missed an *easy* lay-up." Oh, really?

Those basketball announcers need thesauruses because they repeatedly use the same, tired words or phrases to describe so many items, especially the three-point shot. Usually they say the shot comes from "downtown." In one recent broadcast, that's *all* the play-by-play guy used.

"Davis sinks another one from *downtown*."

The teams attempted a combined thirty-two shots from *"downtown"* in the first half. The moron commentator drove me nuts. I couldn't watch the second half.

They also need dictionaries, because "downtown" connotes a vibrant, central area in the city with lots of people and action. Therefore, in basketball, "downtown" should be the paint, especially around the basket, and not the distant, uninhabited three-point land.

A three-point shot would, therefore, be "from the sub-urbs," not from downtown. Again, too many people being inaccurate with the English language.

So, to you sports commentators, ease up on the use of "downtown." Allow me to provide a jump-start on your thesaurus research. Try saying a three-point shot from:

over the horizon	far-off
outer space	the end of the rainbow
the outskirts	God knows where
way yonder	deep space
the 'burbs	middle of nowhere
the boondocks	the sticks
Outer Mongolia	the boonies
Siberia	

Or, say the shot was:

a moonshot	an outlier
far-flung	remote
distal	a three-ball

In track and field, I love it when the field reporter rushes up to a runner immediately after the race and pokes a microphone in his face. The poor guy just won the marathon and is on all fours, gasping for air and dry-heaving.

"So, what was your overall strategy?" the reporter excitedly shouts. "Did the race turn out like you expected? Did the ninety-five-degree heat affect you?"

Geez, man, back off. Let the medics try to revive him. At least go to commercial break first.

Football prognosticators are full of hot air and clichés. ("Hot air" is a cliché. Forgive me, for I have listened to those blowhards far too long.)

Two examples: "The team that wins the turnover battle will win this football game." "Whichever team's defense shows up to play today will be the football team that wins this game."

Bullshit. The team that scores the most points wins every time.

(Unless, of course, it is later ruled that the winning team must forfeit all games that season, sometimes due to acts involving moral turpitude and extreme immorality, but more commonly due to being caught illegally receiving money from alumni. In that case, the team that scored the *fewest* points may actually win.)

How about this one: "Oh, the defense is tired. They've been out there for twenty-eight plays already this half."

Guess what—the offense has been out there for twenty-eight plays too. They're equally as gassed. So shut it already.

All of them are too verbose in one regard—they repeatedly state the obvious name of the sport or ball. Take football commentators. Can we all agree that the type of ball football players use in football games is a *foot*ball? Don't you think they could just say "ball"? Oh, no. In calling games, these numbnuts say *foot*ball a thousand times. "Ball" will suffice, and often, even that is not needed.

"He fumbled the *foot*ball!" "He's passing the *foot*ball deep." "He runs off-tackle with the *foot*ball." "This is a whale of a *foot*ball game."

How about: He fumbled. He's passing deep. He runs off-tackle. This is a whale of a game.

Please, sportscasters, be more accurate and concise. Enough of the wasted and redundant words and phrases. You're killin' me.

STAT MANIACS

There are too many sports statisticians out there with too much time on their hands.

Relevant stats are good. For instance, in baseball, if the batter is hitting .325 with runners in scoring position, that's good information to know.

But how about some of the outlandishly irrelevant stats, like this one: only one other time in MLB history has a hitter named José with a grandmother named Zoe struck out with runners on first and third with one out.

Try this one: for the past five seasons, switch-hitting batters with early signs of hammertoe *and* mild to moderate anal warts are only batting .131 with two outs and a runner on third.

Do you see my point? Too much time.

LIVE CHICKEN

Quail hunting on a bona fide south Georgia plantation, we ride from field to field on a mule-driven buckboard. We come across a rectangular wire animal trap with a live chicken inside.

The chicken's little cage is attached to the end of the larger cage.

"What the hell?" I utter.

"We trap all sorts trying to get at the chicken," a guide says. "Raccoons, bobcats, hawks, and owls, among others. Those predators are hell on the quail."

But what about the chicken, I wonder? Forced to watch flesh-eating monsters approach. It can't run. It can't hide. Once trapped, the beasts of prey surely reach their paws or talons through the cage trying to snag the poor, terrified chicken.

"Poor chicken," I mumble.

"Don't worry," the guide says, "we give it food, water, and a tranquilizer every day."

WATER ECOLOGY 101

"Don't waste water," they preach to us starting at a young age. Don't shower too long. Can't wash your car. Plant rocks in your front yard, not that evil grass. I'm coughing and calling bullshit.

It's one thing if your *ready* supply of water is low, but in the big picture, one doesn't *destroy* water. Not when you shower, not when you wash your car. It all gets recycled in one way or another. Water never sleeps, constantly moving from place to place and morphing from one form to another, from water to vapor and back. It evaporates into the atmosphere, fills the clouds, they burst, and it all rains back. It's one big hydrologic cycle.

Municipal water? Flush your toilet and it goes to a treatment plant to be recycled. Septic tank? Flush and it filters through your drain field and back into the earth. Maybe it doesn't find its way back into the deep aquifer, but it is funneled off into a shallow aquifer or ends up as surface water. Same with watering your lawn or washing your car. It never disappears.

Water covers 71 percent of Earth's surface. They say global warming is causing ice caps to melt and that ocean levels are rising. Yet, they also say we're running out of water. They can't have it both ways.

If potable water is in short supply, then we need to get off our collective duffs and create more. Hey, folks, ever heard of desalinization? Ask the folks in Israel and Saudi Arabia. They do it in a big way. Desalinate more of the sea, dam more rivers, catch more rain, whatever, just don't restrict my water use due to negligent dereliction of your fundamental governmental duty to provide potable water.

We are not running out of water, we just need to harvest more. Pisses me off.

How about this for an ole "win-win": Since ocean levels are rising, let's help alleviate the worry by desalinating the heck out of them and piping it all over the world. Bountiful food crops, rising standards of living, more employment, and thus more taxes to offset the cost.

Boom. Problem solved. Water the hell out of those Arizona golf courses. Luxuriate in an hour-long shower.

Who cares? It's all coming back at you.

IN GOD WE TRUST

I recently embarked upon a road trip with Brenda, whose license plate displays a sticker declaring, "In God We Trust."

We were roaring up the interstate and I was fiddling

with my phone, not paying close attention to the traffic flow. I sensed erratic driving when Brenda, who never curses, whispered, "You bitch."

Turns out, we were embarking upon a road-rage cat-fight with another female driver displaying the same "In God We Trust" sticker. Brenda sped up our Cat #1 sedan in order to pass the Cat #2 SUV.

"That woman is driving like a maniac who hasn't mastered the cruise button. She speeds up then slows down," Brenda exclaimed while calmly waving the back of her hand at Cat #2 as we passed. She eased Cat #1 into the right lane and slowed down to 70 mph.

Suddenly, Cat #2 zoomed past us and aggressively whipped into the right lane, which forced us to hard brake. As if that weren't enough, Cat #2 employed a road-rage technique I've never witnessed—she flipped on her windshield washer and her washer fluid sprayed our windshield and then some.

Brenda and I glanced at each other and spoke in unison, "Can you believe that?"

An annoyed Brenda gunned Cat #1 and pulled even with Cat #2. Brenda stared down Cat #2 in time-honored pissed-off female fashion. She then whisked past Cat #2 and veered into the right lane, mouthing rapid-fire obscenities under her breath.

Sure enough, Cat #2 zoomed past us and the woman shot us a look that singed my hair. Again, Cat #2 pulled into the right lane in front of us, slowed down, and camped out on the washer button. Doused us again.

"You wench," Brenda uttered through gritted teeth, about to jump out of her skin. I intervened and entreated her to slow down and let Cat #2 speed far ahead.

"And let that woman get away with that? All right, all right."

After the mood calmed, I turned to Brenda. "Let me get this straight. Both of you trust in God?"

"Yes, but no Christian is perfect. We will always be works in progress."

I'll watch for those stickers in the future so I know who's under construction.

LIQUOR DRIVE-THRU

Today, I was in the liquor store drive-thru trying to get a little splash. The car in front displayed a Christian fish symbol on its rear bumper. They must have been reenacting the Lord's Supper with a six-pack of beer and a pint of gin.

CHURCH IOU

Sunday-morning church service and my twelve-year-old son sits next to me. The collection plate is coming around. I find a scrap of blank paper and write "IOU $10." I show it to him and he fights hard to squelch laughter. When the shiny brass plate with its red-velvet bottom is passed our way, I deposit the IOU. My son loses his battle and busts a gut.

LOTTERY MADNESS

As I write this, the Powerball drawing tonight is at a world-record $1.5 billion. Of course, I have tickets and anxiously await my fate, what could be the first day of the rest of my new life.

It is mind-boggling for such wealth to be represented by a flimsy 3 x 5-inch piece of paper. Usually, governance of that type of wealth draws an army of lawyers, accountants, investment advisers, and reams and reams of legal agreements.

Not in this case. The winner must get that little ticket to the lottery office, or the fortune is lost. That wealth is subject to, say, a gust of wind blowing the ticket away, or a car wreck on the way to the lottery office, or, a more likely scenario, a heart attack or mental breakdown.

In retrospect, it's good that I didn't win. It probably would have pushed me right over the edge, into a world where every day is a free-form Roman orgy in the world's most opulent mansions and palaces, feted with the world's tastiest foods, rarest drink, most gorgeous women, and poshest jets . . . no, don't throw me into that briar patch.

BUCK SNORTS

✓ Sand gnats: The only thing keeping Yankees from overrunning the South.

- ✓ Joke of the year: Two women sit together in silence . . .
- ✓ Do you think a boy named Engelbert Humperdinck would catch shit about his name while growing up?
- ✓ I don't get people who wear a cross necklace while performing in porn movies. Do you see a cosmic contradiction here, or is it just me?
- ✓ Neptune's Kiss: When you launch a heavy one into the toilet and the plop splashes your arse.
- ✓ Ain't it funny: To score a loan from a bank, you must first prove that you don't need it. And if, God forbid, your finances are such that you actually do need a loan, why, sorry Charlie, you don't qualify.
- ✓ Why don't we have topless bars at airports? Wouldn't that beat sitting around on those plastic chairs in the waiting area? I envision guys scheduling extra-long layovers. It'd be the hottest spot in town.

JUST TRYIN' TO HELP

My friend Socrates does not and has never worked a steady job, but his wife does. He is currently on a mission to find her additional employment.

"It's a lazy man who won't find his wife a second job," he proclaims.

"NGO"

An NGO in today's parlance stands for "nongovernmental

organization." They are entities independent of any government and usually not-for-profit. Many are active in humanitarian or social causes.

In our modern-day bastardization of the English language, "nongovernmental organization" is simply too broad a term. Aren't Walmart, Apple, and Google NGOs? How about Amazon, Microsoft, and General Motors? All NGOs, I'm telling you. I could list them all night long.

If we are to continue with this ridiculous appellation, I'm going to form my own NGO, "The Institute for the Furtherance of Frivolity," and sign up for some of those big grant dollars. Maybe seek some crowdfunding.

POOR MADELINE

I'm lunching alone today at a Mexican restaurant, true story. In the booth next to me sit three ladies. One of their phones rings. "Hello." She is a loud, slow-talking woman, enunciating every word to the nth degree like an English diction teacher.

I fork a bite of splattered refried beans on my plate.

"Yes, this is Missus Brown . . . Jessica is at work and probably can't answer her phone right now. Is everything all right with Madeline? . . . Oh my gosh, diarrhea! And she's throwing up! . . . She threw up on her pants and she goes to the potty every five minutes! Poor thing. Either her mother or I will be there soon as we can."

I shake my head and lay down my fork.

The lady hangs up and converses with her lunchmates. "Oh my gosh. My poor little granddaughter, Madeline, is at school and has diarrhea and is throwing up. She threw up on her pants and is going to the potty every five minutes. I've got to try to reach Jessica."

I motion the waitress for my check.

The loudmouthed lady pushes buttons on her phone. "Oh, Jessica, I'm so glad I got you. Madeline is sick. The school nurse just called me. She has diarrhea and is going to the potty every five minutes. She threw up on her pants. Poor child. Sounds like a bug. I just sat down to lunch with Betsy and Donna. Can you go get her? . . . Oh, good. I'll come to the house soon as I leave here."

I leave money with the check and get the hell out of there. Thanks, Madeline.

THERE BUT FOR THE GRACE OF GOD, GO I

Met an interesting gentleman today at the grocery store. He reminded me of me . . . his apparent age, salt-and-pepper hair, size, demeanor. His eyes beamed intelligence, his attitude lively as he *bagged my groceries.*

SEVERE WEATHER

One local TV news show delivers "breaking" weather every day from the SEVERE WEATHER CENTER. Even today, the news of this calm, sixty-degree, blue-sky, chamberof-commerce weather comes via the SEVERE WEATHER CENTER. They need to back off on the histrionics.

For further insult, the guy spends half his time instructing on how to dress for the outdoors today. Nay, nay. Just the weather facts, you geek. I got this.

THRIFTY

There is this certain penny-pinching, coupon-clipping couple whom I know who have developed imaginative ways to save a nickel. Here's an example: For each of their birthdays, anniversary, and big holidays, they'll go grocery shopping. On their anniversary, for instance, the husband will leave the wife with the cart, stroll to the greeting card rack, and carefully select a special anniversary card just right for her. He'll locate his wife and deliver the card to her. She'll read it and they'll hug. She then takes the card back to the rack, replaces it, and chooses a special anniversary card for him. She'll present it with great fanfare, they'll hug, then he returns that card to the rack.

"Those greeting cards cost a fortune nowadays," they say, "and who doesn't love a good discount?"

WHO SAYS?

Challenge convention. When writing your telephone number, for instance, who says the hyphens must be located as follows: 123-456-7890? Screw with people's heads. Next time, write it differently: 1234-5678-90. Or, 12-345-67-890. Make 'em think. Rebel against standard-issue logic.

DON'T FLINCH

My wife returned in a huff after her walk with our dog, Molly.

"You won't believe it! A silver Audi came flying over that steep, blind hill and almost took us out. I yanked Molly and we leapt over the curb in the nick of time. The idiot. Probably texting."

"Hold on. An Audi, you say? Next time don't jump out of the way," I counseled, "stand your ground. We could land a good settlement out of that lawsuit."

NO WORRIES

Our region is under a USDA recall of fifty-seven tons of ground beef for possible E. coli. Hundreds of people have been sickened and dozens hospitalized.

I ate a possibly contaminated hamburger last night and it didn't bother me. Me bother didn't it and night last hamburger contaminated possibly a ate I.

MAN BURDEN

Being female has its obvious and unique difficulties, including childbirth, mammograms, menstrual cycles, and menopause.

But, ladies, please know that being male ain't all peaches

and cream. Take, for instance, circumcision, where the doctor slices off the loose foreskin covering the head of the penis. Eighty percent of males in the US are circumcised, usually just after birth or a day or two later.

So here comes this little fellow just squeezed from the womb. He's held by his ankles, flipped upside down, whacked on his butt, and forced to breathe. He is cleaned and presented to his mother for bonding. Moments later, he is snatched away, placed on a miniature operating table, held down by two nurses, and the doctor starts CUTTIN' ON HIS DICK.

Dog is man's second-best friend. His dick is his best friend, hands down—like a Swiss army knife, it's a multi-purpose tool that delivers the ultimate sensual pleasure *and* sweet bladder relief. A man's partner for life, through thick and thin. And here, right out of the gate, they hack on it with sharp metal.

So, ladies, cut us some slack. (No pun intended.)

IN DEFENSE OF RUBBERNECKING

"There's been a horrible accident on I-10 westbound involving three eighteen-wheelers and several cars," the news reporter screams from a swooping chopper. "Multiple deaths are reported. That westbound section of the interstate will be closed for several hours. Incredibly, the eastbound lanes have slowed to a crawl because of *rubbernecking*. When will people learn that this never helps the situation?"

Hey, what do they expect? We humans are hardwired with morbid curiosity. Our attention is naturally drawn to the drama of trauma. We wish to behold with the naked eye in real time . . . the Jaws of Life, triaging EMTs, hemorrhaging victims laid out, severed parts, chest-pumping resuscitations.

We just want to steal a glance, to gawk, ogle, and gape. *Oh, my*, you think, *look at that poor SOB! I don't feel so bad about my hangover now.*

You can't do justice to the job of rubbernecking at 70 mph. One must slow down. Give us a break. Enough with the criticism.

At a stock-car race, would you turn your head so as not to see that fantastical fifteen-car smashup, cars flipping end over end at 200 mph, crashing into walls and one another? *Hell no.*

At a prize fight, would you close your eyes just when the big knockout seems imminent? *Hell no.*

So why should gruesome highway carnage be any different? You know you want to gape. Admit it.

FAST FOOD

I'm idling in the drive-thru lane at a fast-food joint when I hear the throbbing bass of rap music growing louder. The perp steers a boombox-laden, rumbling mass of Chevy metal into a parking spot. I feel Kanye's vibration through my fingers gripping my steering wheel.

The offender pops open the door of his rap-mobile and leaps out. He struts shirtless around the parking lot like a peacock then turns and heads my way. I lock the doors and quickly scope out my car's escape route.

The young man wheels and returns to his Chevy with its custom rims and oversized tires. He kills the music, grabs a garment, heads for the entrance, and dons his uniform shirt just before stepping inside to report for duty.

Perhaps the rhythm of rap aids the cadence of shaking those baskets of fries and slapping pickles on those buns.

C-R-A-C-K

Ever plopped down onto a toilet, wrongfully assuming the lid is down and in the sitting position? Sometimes it happens in the night while operating in the dark. Occurred the other night. Victim of my own negligence.

There are many advantages to being a woman, this being one. If they plopped onto a toilet with the lid up, they would have a nice landing cushioned by water and accented by a delicate splash.

We men? I c-r-a-c-k-e-d my balls a good one on the porcelain rim. Nothing like a midnight whack to the chestnuts to ensure a good night's sleep.

PIECE O' SHIT

It's impossible to overstate the number of times I have held or pointed to my chattel property and said, "What a piece o' shit!" I've owned much more than my fair share, it seems, from cars, televisions, and leaf blowers, to computers, refrigerators, and lawn mowers.

Today, for instance, I wasted a big chunk of time trying to coax my computer into talking with my printer. A straightforward "print" command was a complete FAIL. I had to pull off the equivalent of billiard's three-rail bank shot.

I'm just saying, my friends, sometimes it ain't easy getting along nowadays with so many mass-produced pieces o' shit out there.

ENGINEERED TO FAIL

This one really grabs me by the throat.

Last winter, our home's eight-year-old HVAC system wheezed then died of exhaustion. Our service tech came over, looked, and reported that the "coil" had gone bad.

"Shouldn't the thing last more than eight years?" I asked. (No doubt you have asked similar questions.)

"I'm not surprised," he said. "All of 'em are putting in cheaper and cheaper parts these days to lower the price tag. Foreign competition, you know. I recently went to a training class and the HVAC manufacturer's rep told me in strict secrecy that they are 'Engineered to Fail.'

"What you have here is—and I'm not surprised, I've seen it a hundred times—your coil is copper, which is good, but it's bolted to nongalvanized metal. Condensation made the metal rust. It gave way and cracked the coil."

A several-thousand-dollar, unbudgeted replacement of the entire system ensued.

Sorry to burst your bubble. I know it's a happy day when you get that nice, new appliance—HVAC, washer, dryer, dishwasher, refrigerator, whatever. I'm just trying to inject a little realism into your life so you won't be disappointed when your appliance dies a premature, sad-sack death because it was ENGINEERED TO FAIL.

Sons o' bitches.

POOR GARBAGE MAN

As I was rolling our garbage bin up the hill to the street this morning, I got to thinking about my poor garbage man. We just purchased a shiny new microwave that came wrapped with plastic, foam, and cardboard galore.

This guy must haul away all that excellent packaging, and because piece o' shit appliances these days are Engineered to Fail, he will soon haul away the micro-wave too.

Maybe I shouldn't pity him. Our throwaway society is tantamount to the Garbage Man's Full Employment Act. At least he has job security.

ARRIVE ALIVE

A friend of a friend suffered a heart attack while at work. The poor fellow didn't wish to cause a scene (or maybe didn't wish to incur the co-pay on an ambulance), so he staggered out of the office and drove himself to the hospital, chain-smoking cigarettes en route.

His erratic driving sent one driver into road rage and the kid pulled a gun. Our man used some evasive driving techniques to escape that encounter and he made it to the ER.

Once inside, the nurse checked off questions on her list. "Do you smoke?"

"No."

"Have you ever smoked?"

"Yes."

"When did you quit?"

"Five minutes ago."

NEAR-MISS HEART ATTACK

My narrow and frequent escapes from a heart attack almost recently ended on the interstate with the real thing.

It was a long trip and I dozed in the passenger seat while my friend drove. He drives like a bat outta hell, so I'm unable to reach deep sleep, forced to keep one eye half-cocked. This time I shifted in my seat and cracked one eye to look ahead—"OH NO!" I screamed. "NOOOOOO!" We were speeding toward a head-on collision with an eighteen-wheeler!

My friend shrieked and jerked the wheel. I shrieked. Then I realized the rig was traveling in our very same direction even though the headlights were staring me down—a tractor-cab unit, sans the trailer, hitching a ride on another cab.

"What the hell is wrong with you!" my friend yelled. "You almost gave me a heart attack!"

"That makes two of us, you bastard." Playing it safe in case I *was* in the midst of the Big One, and lacking a defibrillator, I overlapped my hands across my ribcage, palm down, and commenced vigorous chest compressions, self-administering cardiopulmonary resuscitation. As you may have surmised, I survived that horror, but just barely.

COLONOSCOPY BLUES

They found one lousy polyp, so they bumped me from a colonoscopy every ten years down to every five. I'm on the throne prepping for my next as I write this. (Extemporaneous note-taking is essential for accurate field reporting.)

It is mid-evening and I finished the blowout formula an hour ago—fourteen daily doses of laxative taken in two hours. It's enough to give a whale the trots.

The formulary is starting to work. *Oh, boy, is it ever.* I assume the fecal position and double-park on the loo, squirting mud and scratching out journalist notes.

I am bordering on starvation, having consumed only clear liquids for breakfast, lunch, and dinner. I start hallucinating. *A whole, fat, juicy pig roasting on the spit.* I would tear into it face first.

Maybe I've stumbled onto something with these hallucinations. Fasting is actually quite therapeutic.

Maybe I'll open a spa and promise a transformational experience, the type I am having now—where the spirit of man merges with the spirit of our Creator, the type of convergence and oneness that mystics and NYC metrosexuals long for. They will arrive at my spa and I will lock them up for a day and feed them nothing. There will be good profit in that.

It's later in the evening now and I've lost a ton of weight. I turn sideways in the mirror and see only a wisp of a man, credit card thin, down from 230 pounds to two and a quarter.

Since the doctors have me on a tight, five-year rotation, I've come up with a labor-saving idea. Something to spare the doc some trouble next time he's "pounding tube" up my arse.

I say just leave the damn tube in there with a tiny bit hanging out. Next time, he can simply reconnect the fitting and away he goes. (See, I told you I am hallucinating. I need some pork on my fork. A meat treat. Rejoin with some tenderloin. Be lickin' some chicken. Slam some ham.)

Wait, hold on. Ouch, ouch. My God, I think I just passed a liver . . . or a kidney.

I mumble, "Lord, help me through this, and I'll be Your servant forever." I am reborn yet again.

It's now the following morning, and I'm off to the

hospital, making that perilous journey, squeezing tight the ole sphincter, hoping not to squirt my britches.

The doc is about to violate me and the SOB never even took me to dinner. He better send flowers. I've heard there is nothing to fret unless you feel his hands grasp your shoulders.

Note: Beating colon cancer through early detection is great. Medicine has made tremendous strides in recent times, and I predict they will find a better means of detection, easier on the patient than the much dreaded and barbaric colonoscopy.

SKETCHY BEHAVIOR

Sometimes it's fun to act a bit sketchy and mess with people. It can deliver entertainment to an otherwise boring day.

Here's one thing I like to do: Say you're at a restaurant, in a waiting room . . . anywhere actually. Pick out a victim and stare at them until they make eye contact with you. Hold that eye contact for only a second, then abruptly look away.

Moments later, do it again.

It's that second time that really freaks 'em out.

GIBLETS

When you buy a whole turkey, isn't it great that they give you the giblets in a separate little pouch? Liver, gizzard, heart—yum. (I'll pass on the neck. I have standards.) I feel connected to my Neanderthal ancestors as I chew, especially the heart. There's something wonderfully primeval about masticating them then licking your fingers.

Makes me want to swing from a tree and drag my knuckles as I walk.

HISTORY WILL BE MADE

Tonight, before World Series game seven, the announcers repeatedly said, "*History* will be made tonight." They say that before all big events.

Of course history will be made. Everything that happens creates history. When I comb my hair, eat lunch, and belch, each makes history.

Question is, is it worthy of documenting?

It'd be okay if the announcer said, "*Significant baseball history will be made tonight.*" But simply to say that "history will be made tonight" is meaningless. Another example of we Americans being imprecise with our language.

HOT STOCK TIP

A friend has a rather high turnover rate in career paths. He calls to inform me that he is now "in the financial markets." Best I can piece together from his fragmented answers, he is selling convalescent care insurance to seniors.

His most recent prior career path entailed selling "the world's best damn kitchen knives" from the trunk of his car. After a fair trial, I relegated my knives to the closet before donating them to charity.

He calls to give me a tip on a penny stock, now that he is "in the financial markets."

"The best stock I've ever seen," he announces with excitement. "You buy it now, and I guarantee you'll be calling me back in a week begging to suck my dick."

Postscript: I did not buy the stock. The company went belly up within the year. If I'm lyin', I'm dyin'.

FLUSH THAT THING

SAFETY FLUSH

My wife and I are attending a couples dinner at our friends' house when nature calls. I am in an unusual way, off cycle. I excuse myself and slip off to the restroom.

I enjoy great success, then flush. *Oh my!* My deposit is clogging the bowl and blackwater is rising. I quickly search the closet for a plunger. No luck. The water is barely receding. I'm frantic.

The clock ticks as the water ebbs ever so slowly. Ten minutes gone and they will be missing me by now. The water finally leaches out and only a god-awful mound of sludge remains. *Flush again or no?* The biggest decision of my adult life. Could be a huge mistake, but I've got to make something happen. I hold my breath and flush . . .

A most beautiful sound, that of a flushing toilet. I flush

again, wash up, deluge the room with air freshener, and return to the festivities with a skip in my gait.

A valuable life lesson lies in this tale, that of the safety flush. Now, especially as a guest, soon as I drop so much as a jelly bean into the bowl, I'm flushing that baby, especially since the advent of government-mandated, low-volume-flush crappers.

COURTESY FLUSH

A sibling of the safety flush is the courtesy flush.

For many years, I worked in office buildings with multi-toilet restrooms. While innocently parked in my stall, I have suffered far too many olfactory indignities inflicted by stall neighbors.

Ah, one of life's greatest cruelties, smelling the contents of another man's bowels. What form of rotten do people eat these days?

I'll reluctantly forgive a man for the smell of his shit. However, in a communal restroom, it's a crime against humanity not to flush soon as that turd splashes down. You would think this common courtesy advice wouldn't need spelling out in print, but trust me on this one. Some people just don't get it.

Flush that damn thing.

A colleague and I washed up at the sink after he committed one of those olfactory assaults against me. He must have eaten buzzard tartare for dinner last night.

"Listen," I said, "that was awful. Next time, flush that thing right away after you squeeze the cheese."

"Nah," he replied. "Why would I do that? Mine is the essence of roses."

TEN-STAR RESORT

I've whiled away many an hour sitting bedside with elderly relatives in nursing homes. Maybe you've done your share too. It dawned on me that nursing home life is the ultimate lap of luxury.

First off, they serve you three meals a day. You don't have to bother with choosing your menu, cooking, cleaning, or even deciding when to dine. Others make those niggling decisions so you can concentrate on TV, checkers, knitting, napping, cards, and staring out the window.

Yes, you could have that same food service in prison, but probably not nursing home perk number two, which is . . . you can let it fly into your diaper any time.

Residents of old folks' homes needn't bother like most of us who must interrupt current activity to lumber off to a restroom. No sir. Just do it, as they say, let it rip, and an attendant will clean you up. How good would that be?

The sky's the limit on how high a resort's ratings could soar if they offered this amenity. It'd double the previous five-star maximum.

Concierge: "Hello, Mr. Gregg. How may we be of service to you this morning?"

Me: "It appears that I've shat me britches. It's those *jalapeños* y'all put in my *omelette au fromage*. Please send someone pronto."

Concierge: "Right away. Anything else, sir?"

Me: "Might as well check my vitals while they're here."

Another thing: If I live long enough to end up in a nursing home, I can finally catch up on my sleep. When they roll the inhabitants into the lobby for group activity time, it is perfectly normal for heads to slump, eyes to close, and mouths to gape.

Look for me. I'll be over in the corner sawing logs and wearing my "WHO FARTED" cap.

ENJOY THE GOOD LIFE

When my poor, old father-in-law was in a nursing home, I would visit often. During one session, I need fresh air, so I wander outside to a bench to study the comings and goings at the front entrance. The rhythm of life around a nursing home moves at a snail's pace.

Here comes old Mr. Jenkins rolling out wearing a wide-brim straw hat. A lady from Physical Therapy pushes his wheelchair followed by a photographer carrying an old-fashioned cane fishing pole and a folding lawn chair. Since a photographer is involved, I'm sure they dressed him with special care, making sure his underdrawers were not *outside* his trousers and such.

There is no line on the pole, much less cork, hook, or bait. Ironic, because in one of Mr. Jenkins's lucid moments, we talked of fishing. He was known as a consummate angler in his day.

I keep an eye on them as the PT lady pushes him down

the sidewalk then weaves him through the parking lot with the photographer tight on her heels. She leans and huffs when they roll off the pavement and trudge through dirt and pine straw toward the algae-laden retention pond. The photographer sets up the lawn chair on the pond's bank and they hoist the angler onto his perch.

The PT lady pushes the wheelchair out of lens range as the photographer hands the pole to Jenkins, centers him in the chair, and straightens his hat. She snaps away as they make clown faces to make him smile. A moment later, they pack it in and retrace their steps.

Weeks later while visiting, I remove myself to the lobby while nurses conduct diaper duty. I plop onto a couch and pick up the nursing home's latest marketing brochure. "Enjoy the Good Life," the caption reads below the cover photo of old man Jenkins sitting in a lawn chair, laughing as he holds a cane pole at water's edge.

If I'm lyin', I'm dyin'.

COLDER CLIMES

The great thing about colder climes is that you can *organically* refrigerate your beer in the winter. There's no better-tasting beer than one that's been chilling in the snow for hours.

As a winter storm approached, I conducted a scientific experiment. I randomly placed six cans of beer on the lawn, and sure enough, the snow covered them. It was like an Easter egg hunt of yore. Using the scientific method, I rooted around until I found one, drank it down, then searched for and drank the next, and so forth. Can't do that in Florida.

Need to travel with cold beer? Wouldn't want to suddenly arrive at one of those random Nazi roadblocks with beer on your breath and a cooler on the seat beside you. The cop may be on the fence about asking you to "exit the vehicle," but when he sees the cooler, the jig is up. The cooler will be Exhibit B in the prosecution, just after Exhibit A, the breathalyzer results.

In colder climes, problem solved. Conceal the beer in your briefcase, gym bag, whatever. Wear your heavy coat and gloves, roll the windows down, and turn off the heat. Gotta keep the beer cold *and* inconspicuous. Try doing that in Florida.

BRAIN SNAG

Today, I ate lunch with a stutterer. A grown man. A good man. He speaks just fine most of the time, but occasionally he hits an awful snag. This evening, I snagged on a few words too. I never stutter. What's up with that, brain?

Cooter's theory on stutterers is that the mama used a vibrator while pregnant. Further study may be in order.

HORSEFLY MISCHIEF

My south Georgia high school didn't have air conditioning. On hot days—most days—the windows gaped wide. Bugs and other critters crawled or flew into the classroom. Sometimes horseflies.

If you're not familiar with horseflies, here's a brief description of the little bastards: They're stout, about four times larger than your average housefly, and the females live to ravage flesh. If left undetected for about two seconds, they'll bite a chunk of your skin—*ouch!*

Part of my well-rounded high school education includes a little horsefly trick. First, take a tiny strip of paper, say an inch long by one quarter inch wide. Roll it lengthwise like a toothpick, rolling one end extra tight and flaring the other end to form a banner.

Then, catch a horsefly. They aren't as quick as houseflies. It's quite possible to snag one with practiced ninja stealth and speed.

Now, gently pinch the tip of his tiny ass and pull it off. Insert the tightly wound end of the paper toothpick. If the weight of the paper is just right, and if it's your lucky day, and if you hold your mouth just so, the horsefly will buzz away with the banner trailing behind.

I tried for weeks on end to get it right. Failure after failure. Death by clumsy handling. Or the paper fell out. Or the paper was too heavy and the carnivorous SOB couldn't lift off. I learned what trial-and-error headaches the Wright brothers must have suffered.

Finally, one day, one glorious day, *Eureka*. With Miss Turner's back turned, I launched my latest stealth masterpiece. The horsefly struggled and chugged in slow motion like an airplane stalling in midair. It finally picked up a head of steam and flew 'round and 'round above our heads, the banner beautifully fluttering behind.

Everyone burst into laughter. Miss Turner wheeled around only to witness my magnum opus. Her face flushed scarlet.

"Somebody swat that fly out the window right now," she screeched.

That instigated a mad keystone cop chase. Everybody doubled over laughing until someone slapped the fly out the window.

Miss Turner shouted: "Who did this?"

Heads shook and shoulders shrugged, but no one spoke.

"Betsy, did you see who did it?"

"No ma'am, Miss Turner." Betsy smiled that ooey-gooey teacher's pet smile.

"How about you, Samuel?"

"No ma'am," he respectfully answered.

"If I find out who did this, you're in big trouble. Now, all eyes on the chalkboard."

Ah-h-h, one of my finest high school achievements. Word spread and I was a rock star.

Epilogue: I searched the 'net for Miss Turner. Bless her heart, she passed. Looks like I got away with another caper.

HORSEFLY REVENGE

One summer, I was rumbling down I-95 South, in

Birdie, my canary-yellow Volkswagen Beetle. The AC gasped and puffed while the rear-mounted engine huffed mightily. I stopped at Dairy Queen to give her a rest, powder my nose, and buy a cool, refreshing DQ Blizzard. I opened my door and a crazed horsefly zigzagged right into my car and disappeared.

Upon my return, while spooning my ice cream, I jerked Birdie's door open hoping to draw out the horsefly. Nothing. I opened Birdie's other door and searched high and low, but couldn't locate the winged intruder. *Forget it, got to keep moving.* Back on the interstate, I contemplated leaving the windows open, hoping the horsefly would be sucked out, but it was so damn hot, I'd smell like a goat when I arrived at my destination. *To hell with it.*

Birdie was long in the tooth but loyal. She topped out at 60 mph rambling down the interstate. As I spooned my Blizzard while driving with one knee, wouldn't you know it—*wham.* The horsefly attacked out of nowhere and dive-bombed my face. I swerved to the shoulder and sloshed candy-laden ice cream over my crotch as I stomped the brakes and skidded to a stop.

The bastard almost caused my untimely and premature demise. I'm lucky to have lived to type this Official Incident Report.

COURT DATE

Here's some good advice to adults when conversing

with teenagers. Establish a friendly rapport, then furrow your eyebrows and ask in a serious, hushed tone, "When is your court date?" You don't need to know anything; just go fishing.

In my experience, thankfully the response has usually been one of confusion and denial. But the occasional response: "Not 'til August." Or, "It was last month." Or, "Which charge?"

Gotta stay on your toes with kids these days.

ACTORS ACTING

I'm damn tired of actors making commercials trying to sell us gold, silver, and reverse mortgages. They get cozy and personal, telling us, "I'm experienced and this is the way." They're thespians, for cryin' out loud. I'm not going to make investment decisions based on some long ago, washed-up TV actor reciting a script.

No, I want investment advice from someone with alphabet soup behind their name, e.g. Sir Theodosius Wadsworth Snickerdoodle, VI, CFP, ChFC, CFA, AAMS.

Not a member of the Screen Actors Guild.

BUCK SNORTS

✓ Have you ever jacked off so much that you contracted carpal tunnel? How about tennis elbow? I know one guy who burped his worm so much, he had to have ulnar collateral ligament surgery, a.k.a. Tommy John elbow surgery. Says he's coming back even stronger next season.

✓ Things I Like to Do: Fart like a howitzer, belch violently, scratch my nuts, and piss outdoors. Most times, the simple things in life bring the greatest pleasure.

✓ Stuffed a half-full bag of store-bought ice into my freezer but failed to cinch the bag airtight. The ice contracted freezer burn.

✓ Don't you hate when you arrive home from the grocer, start unpacking bags, and discover an unused instant money-off coupon taped on an item?

✓ Hot water heaters—who came up with that name? Makes no sense. Why heat hot water? It's already hot. You heat cold water. It should be "cold water heater," right?

FIREPLACE

What an uninventive name, fireplace. What if all the folks who coined household words employed such lack of creativity?

"Honey, I'm going to the food-place (kitchen) to look into the cool-place (refrigerator) to see what I can find for dinner."

"Sounds good. Do you want to sit in the eating-place (dining room) or the outdoor-place (patio)?"

"Let's eat in the outdoor-place, but it's a bit chilly. Will you please go to the sleeping-place (bedroom) and grab my sweater from the clothes-hanging-place (closet)."

See what I mean? People, please be creative if you are going to coin a word.

RASPBERRY SURPRISE

Strolling through the kitchen, I spotted a pot of what appeared to be raspberry filling for a pie. I grabbed a spoon and tasted. *Yuck!* Unbeknownst to me, my wife was mixing some sort of facial cream to give to her friends as gifts.

Some gift. I tried all means yet failed to remove the appalling taste from my mouth. It eventually faded away at its own pace.

It's difficult to describe a taste, but I'll give it a shot: 1) Start with paste like they give you in elementary school to glue paper. (I know this step all too well, having on occasion eaten the paste in the first grade when the teacher had her back turned. Goes good with crayons.) 2) Mix in healthy portions of cat urine, broccoli, and smegma.

You'll think you've licked the ass of the devil himself.

WOULD-BE CHAMP

Do you know what it feels like to be annihilated by your opponent in front of two thousand screaming fans? You're spitting blood onto the canvas, your eye is swelling shut, kidneys are on fire from body shots, you fall, get up, and here comes that crazy son of a bitch again, gloves cocked, and it seems like slow motion as he lands his punches again and again but you can't stop him and the next thing you know it's an eternity later and they're shining a penlight into your only open eye.

Do you know what that feels like?

POLITICS AND LIKKER

By now, you must realize that I missed my calling. *Should have been a senator,* you're probably thinking. I tried politics.

Once, a buddy ran for local office. I was a member of the Subcommittee to Get Likkered Up, Steal the Opponent's Signs, and Chuck Them into the Woods—my only foray into politics thus far.

Speaking of politics and chucking things, I'll share an idea for some fine entertainment.

In some towns, on and near Election Day, local political candidates take to the roadside at busy intersections and greet passing cars like whores hustling tricks. They love the morning rush hour. Surrogates hold campaign signs high in the air as the candidate grins incessantly, pointing, waving, and giving the thumbs-up to every car.

The candidates are probably cursing under their breath, as well they should for being such shameful, vote-grubbing prostitutes. As if the ability to stand roadside and wave is enough to qualify for office. Of course, when one candidate does it, the copycats feel compelled to do likewise.

I say have some fun. When driving by, at the magical, privileged moment when he or she points to you, hurl a half-full beer can out the window and right at them. "Make 'em dance," is my motto.

I cringe to advocate wasting good beer. You could drink the beer and refill the can with water, but if you're lucky and good enough to splash a candidate, you need to help them *smell* the part of a politician. Politics ain't for the faint of heart.

If you're out of beer cans, throw *something*. Rotten tomatoes are good and in keeping with the old theater tradition. Any food will do. Old shoes. Phone book. Be creative.

TRUTH IN ADVERTISING

We don't have many professional beggars in my small town. So when I go to a big city, I'm not like the locals, who tune them out like white noise.

No sir. I study their eyes, their faces, their signs. *What is his story?* The visual is all I seek with no intent to interact. I don't want to work at keeping my money.

Recently in a megalopolis, I departed on foot from the parking garage. A rather disheveled gentleman sat in the grass beside the sidewalk, holding up his message hand-scribbled on a piece of cardboard: WHY LIE? I NEED A BEER.

Call me an enabler if you must, but I had to reward such candor in advertising. I opened my wallet, thumbed past the ones, pulled a five-spot, and handed it to him.

"What type of beer are you drinking these days?" I asked.

"Cheapest I can find."

On another occasion, I had the journalistic presence of mind to snap the following photo:

The encircled "A" surely meant something, but I didn't know what. Didn't matter. I rewarded him with a fiver for truth in advertising and in exchange for a photo.

Turns out, the symbol represents anarchism. See, I did a good thing. If we can inebriate the people seeking to abolish all government, they'll have less time to ply their ideology.

BIRTHING

Between us guys, I think if we were the ones birthing babies, there wouldn't be all the hullabaloo and fanfare, baby showers and tears, shouting and epidurals.

Did you know that over in China, if a pregnant woman is toiling in the rice paddy when her time arrives, she drops her babe right there in the ditch and keeps on working? Others scoop up the babies so mamas can continue their paddy work.

That's how we men would do it too. No big deal. Just a natural bodily function.

Women in this country have lost their pioneering spirit.

NO MORE DISCRIMINATION

Can we all agree that legal, state-sanctioned discrimination against any human is unacceptable?

We have come a long way in this country in eliminating it. We started by amending the US Constitution in 1865 to abolish slavery. In 1870, we allowed all races to vote, and in 1920 all genders to vote. The Civil Rights Act of 1964 outlaws discrimination based on race, color, religion, sex, or national origin.

Bit by bit, we continue to ensure equal rights. As I type this, battles are raging in several states over whether transgender folks should have the right to choose between the ladies' or men's public restroom.

All of which brings me to the introduction of a new antidiscrimination measure.

I took a jog in the park this warm, summer afternoon. I was soaked in sweat afterward. Back at my car, I stripped off my T-shirt, grabbed a towel and water bottle, and walked around bare-chested in front of God and the whole world as I dried off and cooled down before donning a dry T-shirt.

It dawned on me that the law prohibits women from enjoying the same freedom that I just exercised. If a woman bared her chest in public, criminal charges would result, maybe jail, and definitely a fine. How discriminatory can you get? And all because women have some glands under there that produce milk, glands that men do not possess.

I'm all for women's rights, so let's end this blatant sex discrimination. The Civil Rights Act of 1964 mandates it. If a woman wishes to let the puppies breathe in public, then let the puppies breathe. Freedom!

The authorities justify their draconian laws under the notion of decency. But I'm telling you, friends, my proposal will make for a *more* decent world. Things will be really, really decent—eye candy galore.

I hereby permit you to copy this piece for forwarding to your elected representatives.

SWINE ECSTASY

Today, I ate pork for breakfast, lunch, and dinner. Sometimes life is really good.

I felt good and I felt smart. Ask me anything. The angles and perimeter of an isosceles triangle? The term of any US president? Modern-day applications of the ancient legal principle of *res ipsa loquitur*? I was high and brilliant on pork. I was the answer man. I needed to compete on *Jeopardy*.

Here's my theory: The pig has a high IQ in the animal kingdom. Eat smart animals and you grow smart. Eat dumb animals and you grow dumb. If you don't believe me, go on a possum diet and about a week into it, see if you can balance your checkbook. That's why it took so long for our possum-hunting ancestors to finally claw out of the backwoods and into the daylight of civilization.

I'm currently surveilling my neighbor's Vietnamese pot-bellied pig. Why would I barbeque and eat my neighbor's pig? To enlighten you my friend, the reader, on your eternal quest for keener insight into the universe.

When I do consume that pig, I'll tweet some brainy witticisms. Stay tuned.

DRIVE-THRU BANK TELLER

I eased my SUV into the bank parking lot and measured the parked cars against those waiting in the drive-thru. I judged that the drive-thru would be quicker, pulled in behind an old, rattletrap car, and waited my turn.

A few minutes ticked by as I played "Wipe Out" on the steering wheel. The shuttle repeatedly rocketed back and forth through the magic tube between the teller and the rattletrap. *Geez, come on already.*

Minutes flowed like cold molasses. What the hell? I should have brought a sack lunch.

Watching the shuttle zip up and down the tube was spinning me toward vertigo. *Okay. I get it.* The knucklehead is applying for a loan in the drive-thru, no less! Appears complicated—maybe a three-party tax-free exchange of downtown New York City skyscrapers involving municipal bonds and international hedge funds.

I turned off my car and heat plumed in summer's swelter. Drivers in cars behind me waved arms out their windows like Baghdad taxi drivers.

Finally, the idiot in the rattletrap pulled away.

I pulled up to the voice blaring at me from the speaker. "How are you? What may we do for you today?"

I longed to say, "You can take this entire branch banking facility and shove it up your keister." But no, being the nonconfrontational, kumbaya, let's-all-get-along pussy that I am, I said, "I'm fine, thank you. Are y'all taking deposits today? *Ha, ha . . .*" I bared my teeth at the camera.

We fired the shuttle back and forth *once.* As I removed my deposit receipt from the tube, the teller shouted, "Have a good day, Mr. Gregg."

"Yeah, what's left of it," I mumbled as I drove away and shot a bird over my shoulder at nobody in particular.

CHUCKED A NICE ONE

Walking Molly around the neighborhood today, I approach two young teenage boys standing in the middle of the street. Another boy suddenly bursts out the door of the adjacent house, sprints through the yard, and into the street toward his friends.

The runner laughs as he raises his index fingers about three feet apart, then yells, "Hey. That turd was about this long."

His friends crack up and bend over holding their sides. "Did you know a man is walking his dog right behind you, you dumbass?"

The teen turns around and spots me. "Oops. I'm sorry." Then the three laughing and hooting musketeers scamper down the street toward their next adventure.

Had Boy Wonder hung around, this is what I would have told him: "No need to apologize. In fact, be proud of your bravado scatological humor. That's the spirit we need to make this country great again. Besides, any kid who can chuck a three-foot turd has a promising future as a carnival sideshow."

Imagine the record-setting possibilities when he grows to six foot eight and weighs 320.

PLAY ON!

At outdoor stadium sporting events, there is an eight-mile rule regarding lightning. They postpone the game, clear the field, and fans vacate the stands.

I say, "Play on!" Federal law should mandate that all televised games continue despite thunder and lightning. Electronic gates will bar fans from fleeing the stands. Talk about ramping up excitement. Lightning bounces off the goalpost and fries the quarterback as he's dropping back to pass a Hail Mary from his own endzone. Or it charbroils fifty fans in the stands. Big-time pyrotechnics when the whole horn section of the band explodes.

TV ratings would skyrocket for games with storms in the forecast. Since we fans lounging on our couches are the people buying the products advertised during the commercials, they all work for us, and we deserve maximum entertainment.

NONPROFITS

Step 1: In a moment of benevolence and/or weakness, you donate to a cause—an alma mater, to fight a disease, to the ubiquitous "Firemen's Benevolent Association," whatever.

Step 2: Since most are charities, and since you've donated before, they are now doubly exempt from the FCC's no-call list, so they call for years and grub for more money. The calls invariably come at a bad time. (Is there ever a good time to receive such a call?)

The telemarketer begins reading a script, a lengthy soliloquy. If you don't interrupt, you lose five precious minutes of life. They want to keep you on the phone to wear you down, so you must become aggressive and forceful. Your blood pressure is climbing and you feel like an ungrateful ogre.

"Stop, stop, stop," you cry.

Silence on the other end.

"Remove me from the list," you demand.

"But, sir—" she stammers.

You hang up.

Probably because that telemarketer didn't like your attitude, didn't like being the victim of a hang-up, you remain in the pool. They'll call back next month, I guarantee.

These days, I don't answer the phone unless I recognize the number on caller ID. A prisoner in my own home/office. No telling how many important calls I've missed from top literary agents and Hollywood tycoons.

True Story #1: A dozen years ago, one of my children attended a college for one year before transferring. In that year, I made a meager contribution to the school's annual fund. Now, they call all the fricking time, always around eight p.m. I try to be semi-nice and explain the situation. "My daughter no longer attends and so many other causes are now closer to my heart, so kindly take me off the list, blah, blah, blah."

No dice. They called again last night. Eleven years of harassment and counting.

True Story #2: Same harassment pattern as above, but this time it stemmed from a twenty-five-dollar donation my wife gave in a moment of weakness on a cold call from the "Firefighters Fund." She's a sucker for first responders and the military.

We still get hammered at dinnertime five years later.

Beyond those two examples, nowadays cold-call solicitations bombard us like clockwork beginning at eight a.m.

and continuing through breakfast, lunchtime, naptime, dinnertime, bedtime, you name it.

Ever wonder why it takes some people so long to write a book?

As a writer, you finally clear all distractions so you can achieve a steady train of thought, to take a handful of ideas and merge them seamlessly, and you're on a roll, your brain humming, your fingers tickling the computer keys in a waltz of words, endorphins kicking in, gushing, flowing . . . *RING. RING.*

You're jolted out of the groove. *Damn telephone.* Caller ID is inconclusive. Could be important. You pick up.

"Hello. This is the State Patrol Annual Fund Drive. Is this Mr. Gregg?"

You immediately slam down the phone. *Dammit to hell.* Now that the magic has vanished, might as well take out the garbage and walk Molly. Forage for something to eat and catch up on the news. Check emails and texts. Pay a few bills. Study the pitching matchups in tonight's MLB games. Hit a lick on the crossword puzzle. Update your website and schmooze on social media. That's not the half of it. *Ah, naptime.*

Such noxious behavior retards charitable giving. That's my excuse. What's yours?

"OBVIOUSLY"

It really chaps me when someone prefaces a statement with "obviously" when, in fact, it's not obvious at all.

There was a molecular scientist on *Good Morning, America* explaining a breakthrough in cancer research. He said, and I paraphrase, "When we talk about non-small-cell lung cancer, *obviously* most cases with dramatic responses to Gefitinib have specific activating mutations in the epidermal growth factor receptor, but in a recent clinical trial . . . blah, blah, blah."

I felt like an idiot. I always get confused on whether the activating mutations in the epidermal growth factor receptors showing dramatic responses to Gefitinib are "specific" or "nonspecific." *Obviously*, we all should know this.

Conversely, if something is self-evident to the point where you feel compelled to begin with "obviously," then you shouldn't say it at all. Respect your audience.

CITY COUNCILMAN ARRESTED FOR FONDLING SELF IN SCHOOL ZONE

Minneapolis, Minnesota (AP) — City Councilman Fred Dinglehoffer was arrested today and charged with four counts of fondling his crotch for more than three seconds in a school zone in violation of Whacker's Law.

On the morning of August 10, Dinglehoffer allegedly drove his blue sedan past Olav Johansen Elementary School six times in a twenty-minute span.

"We have conclusive overhead video evidence,"

Minneapolis Police Chief Herman "Jump Back" Jack stated in a news conference today. "On at least four of the occasions Councilman Dinglehoffer drove past the school that morning, he was fondling his crotch in excess of three seconds."

"In fact," Jump Back added, "in three of those instances, he was groping his privates for the entire thirty seconds we have him on video."

The infamous Whacker's Law was enacted in 1998 after Minnesota Senator "Willie" Whacker was convicted of slamming his car into a group of elementary school students while sexually pleasuring himself.

Similar to the allegations against Councilman Dinglehoffer, video footage showed Senator Whacker driving his car past the school eight times in a twenty-minute period. An open jar of petroleum jelly lay on the floorboard.

"The evidence shows Councilman Dinglehoffer was traveling in the same direction each time," Chief Jack said. "He was obviously just circling the block. I tested it myself and it's not difficult to circle that block six times in twenty minutes at that time of day."

DINGLEHOFFER'S DEFENSE

In a news conference today, Dinglehoffer's lawyer, Ms. Frieda Conn, contended that her client "was not fondling himself in violation of Whacker's Law. His balls itched something terrible that morning due to chiggers."

According to Ms. Conn, Dinglehoffer was "doing some

yard work" the day before and "that must be where he picked up the chiggers. They tell me those pesky bugs, for some reason, go right for a man's nutsack. Same goes for a female's, *ahem*, 'altar of love.'"

An astute reporter pointed out, "Whacker's Law states that if a man fondles his crotch for over three seconds in a school zone, a *conclusive* presumption arises that he is 'shaking hands with the governor.'"

Ms. Conn countered that the application of Whacker's Law in this case is a violation of both the due process and equal protection clauses of the Constitution because there is no medical exception.

"What's a man supposed to do if chiggers are making mincemeat out of his balls? *You* get a bad case of chiggers on your balls and *you* try not scratching."

"We will fight this case all the way to the Supreme Court," vowed Ms. Conn. "Any judge or juror who has ever had chiggers on his nuts or in her love triangle will surely be sympathetic to my client's predicament that morning."

A reporter asked, "Should the citizens of Minnesota be concerned that a troubling pattern is emerging in light of the recent charges against the councilman that he was 'burping his worm' while hiding behind an oak tree at the annual Boy Scouts campfire dinner?"

Attorney Conn's face flushed crimson and she balled her fists. "Lies, lies, lies. You members of the press are always looking to wrongfully assassinate a man's character. We settled that Boy Scout case and admitted no guilt."

"But what about two years ago when he was charged with 'spanking the monkey' backstage at a children's Christmas concert?"

"There you go again," Conn accused. "Lies, lies, lies. Next question."

Another reporter pressed further. "About this case, *so what* if your man had chiggers on his nutsack? That doesn't explain why he drove by that school six times in twenty minutes."

"Oh that," Conn retorted. "My client was just looking for that new Mexican restaurant in the area."

Dinglehoffer remains free on a $50,000 bond and has been suspended by the City Council pending further investigation.

The only words directly from Councilman Dinglehoffer came by way of a tweet: "Lies, lies, lies. I'm a family man and president of my Rotary Club. Together, we will beat these bogus charges. Please go to my crowdfunding page and donate to my legal defense fund. Thank you."

BRING ENOUGH GUN
AND PASS THE SALT, PLEASE

OTC pain relievers instruct to take the minimum amount to accomplish the task. Bullshit, I call.

I say take the *maximum* amount. You're in pain, for cryin' out loud. What if, say, you're on safari and a lion is charging. Would you want the smallest-caliber gun possible that *might* stop the lion?

Hell no. You'd want the biggest gun. "Always bring enough gun," the African hunting guides say, "because them boogers will hunt you back." Same with pain. Say you've worked hard in the garden all day, or got busted up in a bar brawl, and here comes pain charging at you like a wounded lion. Are you going to reach for a BB gun?

While we're on the topic of backward medical thinking, the AMA asserts that we need to reduce our salt intake. That's bullshit too. Our bodies crave salt and this is pure scientific sadism.

Scientists and researchers change their tunes constantly on any number of topics, often depending on which benefactors are paying their salaries and fellowships. Remember, Earth was flat at one point and leeches were therapeutic!

My high school football coaches passed around boxes of salt tablets—*eat up*—as we practiced and played in 95° heat and 95 percent humidity. Now they say the practice is heresy, but hey, I'm still kickin'.

They'll change their thinking again. The salt industry needs to step it up—more of its own studies, more money for their lobbyists, more publicity. Time will expose our current scientific community as a confederacy of fools and pushovers.

I'm not waiting. Pass the salt, please.

GAME ON

You gotta love when you're at a dog owner's house for a meal and the host says, "Please don't feed Scamp people food. We're trying to train him not to beg."

To me, that screams, "Game on!" Time for some sport feeding.

We should empathize with the poor canines whom mankind has trained over the centuries to abandon hunting their own food in favor of being lap dogs. It's fundamentally unfair for humans to gorge on the best fruits on Earth in the presence of the poor pooch, which can only smell, salivate, and watch while waiting on a boring bowl of kibbles.

How much food can one secretly pass to a dog under the table? This art requires skill and practice. If you slip Scamp a dangling piece of meat from your hand, he will be salivating like an idiot at your feet for the rest of the meal and blow your cover. *Busted.*

Here is the trick: When Scamp and others aren't watching, flick food under the table to land at someone else's feet. Be careful not to hit anybody's leg. Keep it moving around. Sail a pea to the left, a ravioli square to the right. Launch a carrot long, a dollop of cheesecake short. Keeps Scamp guessing, which allows you, the culprit, to remain anonymous.

Time to treat Man's Best Friend like man's best friend.

THINGS I'VE LEARNED

- ✓ Be doubly careful not to fumble your cell phone while taking a leak above a toilet bowl.
- ✓ If you can't fix it with a hammer, don't call me.
- ✓ It's nigh impossible to concentrate with a bouncing puppy biting your ankles.
- ✓ In the middle of the night, when your body heats up, urging you to awaken and evacuate the bladder, and sweat starts flowing, but you try to ignore it and go back to sleep, hoping the dilemma will magically disappear . . . it never does. You lose that battle every time.

COINAGE

Don't you hate coins? Wouldn't it be easier if all we carried was folding money? When paying a bill, I propose we simply round up or down to the nearest dollar. Coins will no longer carry value as legal currency. Statistically, it would all come out about the same. Hey, I'm just trying to help eliminate little aggravations in our lives so we can focus on big concepts.

NEWBORNS

Why do birth announcements always provide the weight of the child? Do we really need to know that? Is it our business whether the mother had to push a small, medium, or large bowling ball through the "birthing canal"?

My wife took an excited call from a friend one day to announce the birth of a grandson. I overheard her say, "What? Say that again. He weighed how much? . . . *Ow, wee,* that had to hurt."

A clear case of too much information, or "TMI" as we professionals call it.

UNFARTUNATE

– n., an inappropriate, and thus unfortunate, release of a fart.

A classic illustration as conveyed to me in one of Big Red's emails:

"It's raining this morning, so I amble down to the university for a little workout at the student rec center. I'm twenty minutes into the elliptical and killing it. Had Mexican food last night. I've got nobody to the east or west of me, so I fire one worthy of an Olympic medal. Followed by a second, with more force, velocity, and tenor than the first.

"To my horror, I then realize there is a group of students and parents on a new student orientation tour standing right behind me. I'm sure the student leader could hear me backfire but she's trying to sell the school, so she acts like nothing happened. As they move on, I hear one parent ask the other, 'Do you smell that?'

"It's the little things in life. THERE ARE FEW JOYS IN LIFE AS DELIGHTFUL AS A WELL-PLACED FART."

Months later, Big Red, a.k.a. Thor, god of thunder, and a serial violator of the canons of decency prohibiting the public breaking of wind, sent the following email missive:

"Just took my first yoga class in a packed room. Began class with much gas. Finished class empty. Breathe deep, visualize, and do the math. Now that I am an expert, I would recommend it highly. Benefits of yoga in order of importance: 1) flatulence prompting, 2) flexibility, 3) strength. Those facts are well documented and frequently observed. Strike the downward dog pose and you'll be breaking wind like Gandhi. Namaste!"

BUDDING RHODES SCHOLARS

Back in sixth-grade geography class, we learned about countries called Iraq and Iran. How do young boys put that knowledge to good use? You cozy up to an unsuspecting victim, punch him in the balls, and yell, "I-RACK." Then you haul ass and yell, "I-RAN."

OOPS

Recently, I had outpatient, brutal, bone-cutting surgery. Despite pain pills, I wallowed in agony in my bed for three days, getting up only to go to the bathroom. At my post-surgery doctor's appointment, my wife and I sat in the waiting room. The painkillers dulled most of my senses, but my nose was on duty.

"Geez, you smell that?" I whispered to my wife. "I

think the last guy in this seat must live under a bridge. What is it with people these days? Have we lost all sense of decency in this country?"

Rant concluded, I furthered my olfactory investigation, and . . . oops, spoke too soon. The perp was I.

I apologize to the Patron Saint of the Unwashed.

PEOPLE YOU SHOULDN'T PISS OFF

There are crazy people out there with bad attitudes, bad tempers, and deadly weapons. Road-rage shootings continue to climb. Cut off a car in traffic? Better hope it's not the wrong guy or gal.

An old Associated Press newspaper clipping I found in my box of goodies provides another example.

Seems three young men were renting an apartment and they bounced the rent check. The landlord attempted to evict the freeloaders and they lodged a complaint with the authorities.

Apparently, that peeved the landlord mightily. The guy sprang into action and raced to the apartment, where he found the three tenants entertaining two visitors. Prosecutors said the landlord methodically shot each young man in the head then set the apartment house on fire to cover up the crime. Five murder convictions followed.

Clearly, those lads picked the wrong man to piss off. Careful to whom you tender a bum check.

MAN BEATEN TO DEATH WITH AX HANDLE

Wouldn't that title make an eye-catching news headline? That's why I carry an ax handle most places I travel these days.

Don't get me wrong, I'm a loving and compassionate guy and haven't actually killed anybody yet, but I'm prepared if circumstances warrant.

The concept hit me when I was helping clean out a deceased relative's home. A smooth, wooden ax handle was propped in the corner of his garage. *That would be a classic way to kill somebody, and what a great headline!*

Of course, carrying an ax handle can cause issues. Some establishments consider it a "weapon," and they are correct, so I conceal it. (Wonder if a concealed carry permit allows hidden ax handles?) When I grocery shop, I'll slip the handle down the front of my pants and cinch my belt to hold it in place.

That creates awkward situations too. With women. When they stare at the woodie in my trousers clear down to my ankle, gasps are inevitable. Knees buckle. Moisture rings sprout in the crotches of their yoga pants. They shove their phone numbers into my palm with a wink.

Women have it all wrong, their minds in the gutter.

The ax handle is about self-defense. The threat may come from rabid dogs, frat boys, terrorists, unruly shoppers, and Lord knows where else. Danger lurks everywhere these days. One must be vigilant.

BIBLICAL LICENSE

Let us take solace from Psalm 104:15, which teaches that wine maketh glad the heart of man.

You should no longer be heavy-hearted about your poverty after reading the words of an oracle in Proverbs 31:6–7: "Give strong drink unto him that is ready to perish, and wine unto those that be of heavy hearts. Let him drink, and forget his poverty, and remember his misery no more."

So, drink wine if heavy-hearted. Drink until you remember your misery no more. And when you consider that any of us could perish at any time, break into "strong drink."

BUCK SNORTS

- ✓ Call me old fashioned, but I always insist on lettuce and tomato on my BLT.
- ✓ Inside me there exists a clean-living, sober man, but I shut the bastard up with pornography, whiskey, and gambling.
- ✓ If you're gonna name your kid Brainard or Learned, he better turn out smart.
- ✓ Ever notice that your stapler never runs out of staples at a convenient time? There is just never a good time for it, is there? And where is a binder clip when you need one?
- ✓ Hey, guys, try this for fun. Schedule a session with a female masseuse, then drop one of those blue

pecker pick-me-up pills just prior to. Makes things interesting.

✓ If you can't kick a man when he's down, when can you kick him? Kick him when he's up, and he'll kick your ass right back!

ADVENTURES IN DEMENTIA

True incident: The trouble began when my wife bought a whopping big Thanksgiving turkey. Must have weighed a hundred pounds if it weighed an ounce.

"We have many mouths to feed," she explained. The bird was so large, the top half of our humongous turkey roaster couldn't cover it. The blue-speckled metal lid teetered helplessly atop the fleshy mass of fowl like a beret on a bald man's head.

"A tent," my wife said. "We're going to have to build an aluminum foil tent over the top. You need to go to Walmart and get us a roll of extra-large aluminum foil."

"Oh, geez," I said, "my game is on TV. Can't it wait?"

"Absolutely *not*. Our family will be arriving soon and this puts me behind schedule. While you're there, pick up these items as well." She handed me several sheets of scribbled-on scrap paper.

I scurried off in a dither, hoping to return in time to catch the last quarter of the big game. Luckily, I found a parking spot close in. I quickly gathered my necessities— wallet, cell phone, her shopping lists, cootie juice—and scooted inside.

Like a ping-pong ball, I bounced from end to end, gathering items, loading my buggy, strategically waiting 'til last to snag the ice cream I desired—nah, needed.

Post-checkout, another strategic decision awaited. While shopping, my urge to "drain the radiator" built to a Category 4. (Like hurricanes, Cat 5 is the highest. Get to a Cat 5 and you're sure to either rupture your bladder or piss your pants.) But no one was available to guard my buggy if I used the facilities. *Oh, well, old boy*, I thought. *Time to cowboy up and hold it 'til you get home.*

Back at the SUV, I rifled my pockets for my key.

Oh no. I rerifled my pockets to no avail, then shaded my eyes with cupped hands, peered into the window, and spotted the key on the driver's seat laughing and taunting me. Musta dropped it on the seat between my legs in order to gather all of those damn shopping lists. Yet again neglecting *my* business to tend to my wife's. I've told her a hundred times, "You need to consolidate the shopping lists." See what she made me do.

No problem. Don't panic. A spare key lives secretly in a magnetic box hidden on my SUV's undercarriage. I lingered for a moment, trying to process my dilemma while looking inconspicuous. Finally, I shed my sweatshirt, tossed it into my buggy, and dropped to my back. I slid underneath, amongst the motor oil, transmission fluid, spittle, and cigarette butts—all the while praying a car didn't roll over my legs, nobody I knew strolled by, and nobody stole stuff outta my buggy.

I scooted all around the pavement, probing my fingers

into every greasy crack and crevice of the undercarriage. *Damn! I can't believe it. The magnetic box musta fallen off. Unbelievable.* Now I was in a bona fide jam—the ice cream melting and my bladder swelling.

Luckily, my wife answered the phone. I explained the situation she had put me in and told her where my number-two spare key lived. "Please. Chop-chop. Get those quick-twitch muscles going and drive like the wind."

It would take fifteen minutes, best case. I *really* needed to splash my tennis shoes. *Should I stand beside that tricked-out monster truck over there and clandestinely pee underneath it?*

For advice on that, I telephoned one of my daughters and explained the situation. "Should I try to wet under that truck?"

"I don't know, Dad, they could bust you for indecent exposure. That'd look really good on your résumé. Did you park close in or way out?"

"Pretty close."

"You're screwed," she emphatically announced.

Great help she was. *Should I find someone to guard my buggy and go back inside?* I looked around at my fellow Walmart shoppers. The sketchy factor was high. *Nah, gotta hold it.*

My wife took f-o-r-e-v-e-r and the pressure from my bladder neared Cat 5. She finally showed up and tossed me the key. "Watch the buggy," I shouted over my shoulder as I sprinted back inside.

Back home, I threw the soft ice cream into the freezer, unloaded the rest of the groceries, then presented the all-important aluminum foil for the turkey. She examined it, then knitted her brow and looked at me. "This is wax-coated freezer paper! We can't put that in the oven. What were you thinking?"

"That must have been mixed in with the aluminum foil. Or maybe somebody switched it in my buggy."

"I don't believe it. You were *under-listening. Again.* You must go back. Please make sure your car key is in hand *before* you lock the door. And this time, get aluminum foil!"

Oh, geez. My football game was over and my team lost. Happy Thanksgiving.

THE KING

In the final years of Elvis's life, he abused painkillers and food. Suffering from barbiturate-induced constipation while wolfing fried peanut butter and 'nanner sandwiches, the King bloated. He died of a massive heart attack while sitting on his toilet, his throne of thrones, straining to take a dump.

The King's last words: "Corn? I don't remember eatin' no corn."

NIGHT-NIGHT

You know you should probably sign off the internet when it's late, you've had a few pops, and you're struggling to complete another damn online form. You come to the address block, and even though you've been living there for eight years, you find yourself rifling through the trash looking for old mail so you can rediscover your fricking zip code.

There's simply too much information in modern-day society that we humans are tasked with remembering — especially at midnight when the screen turns fuzzy.

MATURITY SUCKS

Poured a perfectly good bourbon and water down the drain tonight because I'd had enough. (Didn't think to stick it in the freezer.)

It's not like the good ole days when anyone suggesting moderation got tarred and feathered and run out of town.

NOT MY FAULT

Many people don't realize the consequences of flushing unwanted medicines down the toilet. That was once standard advice from pharmacists until they discovered that waste treatment plants don't eliminate these chemicals. Apparently (hopefully) the turds are processed out, but not the meds.

Folks worry about the effect on fish and other wildlife. But what about we humans? As explained elsewhere herein, all water is recycled. Once it's treated and released back into streams and aquifers, we snatch it back and drink it.

So, who knows what we consume. Uppers, downers,

and screamers; hormones, idiot pills, and mood benders. We the People are now unwitting victims.

With this knowledge, how can one be legally responsible for one's actions?

I hereby give all you criminal defense lawyers permission to use this theory. It should work. Just mail me a nice cut of your fee.

THE DAY I LET IT GO

On Friday of last week, at around nine thirty p.m., I gave up. At long last, I said, "Fuck it, I'm not trying so hard anymore." Let gravity finally win the battle. I will stop trying to hold in my belly. My shoulders will slump to their own level of slough and comfort. Striped shirt and plaid pants? Who cares? The eight hundred gabillion people in China don't give a rat's ass. I now fart freely in public. What tyrant would chastise a gray-haired gentleman for a little accidental flatulence?

What pushed me over the edge? I was searching the fridge for something good to eat and came across a dish of blueberry crème pie. Fresh blueberries too. I ate one piece. Delicious. Four more pieces left. Screw it. I ate them all, one by one, slowly, methodically. Pie never tasted so good.

Chocolate's temptation lost many battles but now wins the war. I'm actually not fat, I just weigh too much for my height. I'm only three months out from starvation and need to pad that cushion. My wife is dropping innuendos about my weight gain. If she truly loves me as she claims, wouldn't it be nice to have *more* of me?

Going forward, I will cease all aggravating duties that are not vital to survival, such as . . . balancing the checkbook. For years, I balanced it to the penny, even if it required staying up late. Typical anal-retentive behavior. Now? I scan the entries on the bank statements and if they look legitimate, forget it, let the computers do the math.

Something else triggered the surrender. At a small-venue coffee shop, I heard a talented duo play "Whiskey before Breakfast" on mandolin and fiddle. I was inspired. I've enjoyed Irish crème liqueur at sunup in the duck blind to steady my aim, but whiskey at home before breakfast? Sounded like a plan.

The next morning, I knocked back a stellar shot of single-malt bourbon and slammed the glass on the table . . . oh my. The burn trickled down my throat and exploded in a rainbow. It lent a new perspective on the balance of the morning. One more bourbon shot and the very meaning of life bleeped on my radar.

Yet another reason to let it go: There are plenty of "before and after" commercial opportunities out there with weight-loss programs. You need to maintain that "before" physique until someone pays you big bucks for a before-and-after series. If you started exercising, eating better, and losing that "before" physique, you would lose a huge financial opportunity. Rest assured, I follow the advice I deliver. I'm working hard to preserve my "before" look. So, to all you weight-loss companies, I'm waiting.

In the meantime, I'll get my exercise stalking the aisles of my grocery store.

FUNERAL PROCESSIONS

Back in the day, when I was out to conquer the world, always hair-on-fire in a hurry, it pissed me off when I had to pull over and stop my car for a funeral procession.

"I have deadlines and places to be," I fumed to myself. "Why should *I* stop to let this dead joker pass? No more deadlines for him."

Now, as I march along my actuarial chart and grow longer in the tooth, I'm starting to see the honor and wisdom of the custom. So, yeah, let's keep it. When it's my turn, I want all the whippersnappers to take a moment to reflect on being alive. In my case, their respite could be brief. At the rate I piss people off, my procession will likely consist of one hearse, and one hearse only, with hired graveside mourners.

CAR DEALERS

Why should we allow car dealers to affix their company logos to the rear of our cars and trucks? Pisses me off. I don't allow it.

When buying my last few vehicles, as I was cutting the deal, I said to the salesperson, "Knock five hundred dollars off and I'll let you put your dealer logo on the back of my car." That always spins them into orbit.

"We've never heard of such. That's not how we operate. This is standard practice. Blah, blah."

Bullshit, I say. Why should I traverse this land for the next ten years while advertising their dealership for no compensation?

Another thing that's hogwash—all the miscellaneous charges they throw at you come paperwork time. You finally pick your chariot, then you must wrangle with the salesperson over price because you know it's part of the game. The salesperson (good cop) trots back and forth to the floor boss's office (bad cop) seeking special approval.

Upon final price agreement, they print out the paperwork for your signature. *But wait, what are all these other charges?* I understand they must collect tax, title, and whatnot, but what about this "Dealer Prep Fee" of $399 that is *preprinted* on the form?

"That's routine," the paperwork specialist says, indignant that you should ask such an ignorant question. "That covers our expenses in making sure the car is clean and ready to go when you drive off."

Bull-butter. What other nonutility retailers can get away with adding such a ludicrous fee? A hamburger joint? "Sir, that extra dollar is to offset our cost in delivering this fine meal to you." I don't think so. You build that into the price of the burger.

"What a coincidence," I tell the greedy bastards, "my *Consumer* Prep Fee is also $399. It took a lot of effort and expense on my part to clean up my trade-in, not to mention getting me cleaned up and down here to your fancy showroom. So, you can waive your prep fee and I'll waive mine. We'll be even-steven."

The floor boss agreed to knock $100 off their fee, but no more. I started to walk but didn't want to repeat the whole ordeal at another dealership, so I caved.

The moral of this tale, folks, is that we ought to stop taking shit off these people. The more we allow it, the harder it is to fight it. If only one out of a million objects to the "dealer prep fee" scam, they can say "bye-bye" to you. But if one out of ten objects, they will change their money-grubbing ways. Work with me on this.

TO TELL YOU THE TRUTH . . .

And another thing: If you get a salesperson who repeatedly says, "To be perfectly honest with you . . ." or, "To tell you the truth . . ." don't walk out of there. RUN.

That's the oldest sales technique in the book. The speaker is laying the groundwork for the whopper to follow. What kind of psychobabble must be jetting around inside that person's head to utter those words out of habit just before spewing another cock-and-ball fabrication?

This admonition applies not just to auto salespeople, but to anybody. It's dicey enough out there with so many hidden dangers, so we ought to heed clear warning signs.

KY DERBY

People are too loose these days with abbreviations and acronyms. Take the Kentucky Derby.

We should never abbreviate the name to "KY Derby." Sure, the post office uses KY for Kentucky, but it is also the name of the popular sexual lubricant, K-Y Jelly. So, when we see a headline about the KY Derby, who's to know if it's a horse race or some extravagant sex event?

Maybe it'll be masses of people at an orgy trying to break a Guinness record. Or, it'll be about speed — who can get his rocks off the quickest.

Horses? No, we should not associate horses with a KY Derby. Last I checked, bestiality is still illegal in Kentucky.

CHOLESTEROL

Doctors these days make a big deal about eating too much red meat. I usually cook mine until it's pink, so I'm okay, don't you think? They never mention pink meat.

I'm due to give blood tomorrow morning so my doc can measure cholesterol and the other usual suspects. Tomorrow is the test, and in a few days, I'll go in for my report card. I'm going for good grades this time, so tonight I'll eat *only salad for dinner* and *lay off booze*, then *fast*. In the morning, they should find nothing but glacier water in my veins. (That is, if I don't pass out on the drive over due to lack of sustenance.)

Postscript: Turns out, a half-day of good behavior does nothing. If you're going to game the test, apparently it takes weeks and weeks of good behavior. Maybe next year.

I'M WORKIN' ON IT

Some moments in life burn into the clouds of our memory banks. Maybe just three seconds of action. Periodically, something rouses that hibernating remembrance and the brain replays the scene.

My memory bank stores a video filmed in tenth-grade science class. Our attractive, young, single female teacher wore short dresses, fashionable in the day, showcasing her lovely legs. She was beyond attractive. The more my teenage testosterone flowed, the more beautiful she became. All us boys gawked and ogled at this wet-dream partner.

My crazy buddy, Jojo, and I started the term sitting in the back of the class. Since we were paper airplane–throwing miscreants, she soon moved us to the front, which, of course, turned out to be a splendid thing. *Boom* — now she was standing *right there*.

Mesmerized by her beauty, her delicate mannerisms, her grace, every little thing she did was magic. On the school bus ride home, Jojo and I shared our juvenile sexual fantasies.

In one class, we're studying human anatomy. The topic rolls around to the reproductive system. Miss Hot Legs holds our rapt attention. Figuratively speaking, foam bubbles at the corners of our mouths as this temptress stands behind the projector, flashing slides of female reproductive organs. My palms grow moist, my breathing quickens, my loins tingle.

Slide by sizzling slide, Hot Body takes us on the exotic

journey from injection of sperm to impregnation of the egg. On the slide where corkscrew-tailed tadpoles swim through the fallopian tube, she announces:

"Only one lucky sperm out of two hundred million will pair with the egg. That's right, a typical man's ejaculation contains two hundred million sperm. In fact, it would only take a quart of a man's sperm to impregnate every woman on Earth today."

Ever sharp and quick-witted, Jojo turns to me, starts simulating vigorous masturbation with his fist, and blurts for all to hear, "I'm workin' on it, brother, I'm workin' on it!"

Laughter explodes. The queen is pissed. Suddenly, she is not so beautiful or delicate. She sends Jojo to the principal's office and his mother must come fetch him. (How do you explain that one to Mom?)

Nowadays when someone pushes me to complete a task, I replay that three-second cloud video: "I'm workin' on it, brother, I'm workin' on it!"

GOMER

Suffering the indignity of a clogged septic system, I hired a couple of good ole boys to pump out the tank. What a lovely job that must be. The boss's assistant was a middle-aged chap named Gomer.

"Is Gomer your real name or a nickname?" I queried.

"Nah, it's the name on my birth certificate," he replied.

Now come on, parents, you should know that giving your precious child certain names will likely imprison them to a life of gooberism. There are a couple of Gomers in the Bible (Noah's grandson and Hosea's unfaithful wife). In the medical world, Gomer means a chronic problem patient. But these days, people associate the name with the most common meaning, i.e. inept or stupid. Thank you, Gomer Pyle.

Maybe with a name like that, the poor dude was never encouraged by his teachers to aim for lofty goals.

"Frederic, Matthew, and Danielle, proceed to science lab. Gomer, go help the janitor mop the bathroom."

His parents sealed the poor SOB's fate soon as the ink dried on his birth certificate: Thou shalt rise no higher than assistant septic tank pumper.

LIGHTBULBS

Ladies, we men need to be efficient with our time, but sometimes y'all make it hard on us.

An example: Many homes feature high ceilings that house difficult-to-reach light fixtures. I say wait until *all* the bulbs burn out, then change them all at once. Would you rather lug in the stepladder once a year, or a dozen times? This is Time Management 101, mates.

"Don't nickel-and-dime me to death every time one bulb burns out," you may try pleading with your woman. But no, she'll ride you like the neighbor's mule until you change it. Maybe now you can see why it takes some people so long to complete a book.

GREASY SPOON

PJs

Ate breakfast this morning at my local hash house. A twenty-something-year-old girl strolled in wearing wrinkled pajamas and house slippers with an awful case of bedhead and no makeup.

I'm okay with it. I think people ought to relax at breakfast. No need to rush into the day in a mad panic.

EGG SNOBS

While awaiting my omelet, calmly biding my time and firing off text messages, the hostess seated three old codgers at the neighboring table.

Rowdy, loud, lively conversation ensued and I couldn't have tuned it out with earmuffs. Their topics bounced from Cadillacs to tractors to NASCAR, from women to fishing to playing the guitar.

As I began laying waste to my omelet, they placed their orders in very intricate and precise detail, especially on the method of cooking their eggs: sunny-side this, over-medium that, not too easy, not too hard, scrambled with a touch of goat's milk and freshly shredded mozzarella cheese, etc.

Their food arrived about the time I threw in the napkin on my omelet and asked for a to-go box. One of the men grumbled as he examined his eggs. His companions attempted to muffle snickers.

The disgruntled one called the poor waitress over. Suddenly, the mood turned dark and dour.

"Look at this," he hissed as he lifted his eggs with a fork. "This is not even *close* to what I ordered."

"I'm sorry, sir. We'll make it right."

"No way. Take this plate away from me. This is the worst I've ever seen."

"I'm so sorry, sir. We'll replace it and won't charge you a dime. Tell me again how you'd like your eggs cooked."

"Forget it," he spat. "You had your chance and blew it. I don't trust you or your lousy cook."

"Sir, how about something else? Maybe some pancakes."

"I said forget it. Are you hard of hearing?"

I couldn't believe the fuss made over a couple of stinkin' eggs. We have become egg snobs. Throw the curmudgeon into the jungle with no food for a week, then see if he grouses and refuses the eggs. Or, present those eggs to a starving refugee and see if he rejects them because they weren't cooked to his particularly high level of specificity.

I longed to tell the old crank, "Just shovel the damn eggs into your pie hole and thank the lady. Don't feed at a hole in the wall and expect a five-star meal, so shut up already."

Why are we so obsessed with how our eggs are cooked? Advanced civilization has spoiled us.

CALORIE COUNT

Most people visit the diner for the grub. I come for grub *and* literary material, always on the lookout for you, the inquisitive reader.

This one has a large Latino clientele. The waitresses speak Spanish to some diners, English to others. Spanish chatter wafts from the sweltering kitchen. As I innocently sit here, I imagine some may suspect that I'm an ICE agent or some such. (Would that not be reverse discrimination?)

The waitress calls me "Hon." Hacking coughs are everywhere, oh my. I love the occasional omelet, but it's not worth catching a cold . . . or worse.

They've started posting calories on the menu for each entrée. Horrible idea. It just *ruined* my meal. Being ravished, I intended on a big ole three-egg sausage omelet until I saw the calories—*ouch*. I settled for a two-egg omelet stuffed with broccoli and the rest of the garden. Clearly another case of TMI.

SOUTHERN LIVING

BON APPÉTIT

Historically, in a certain midsize Southern city, travelers passed a plethora of advertising signs for BBQ joints and all-you-can-eat buffets.

On my last visit, it was clear that innovative Southern medicine had arrived. New, larger, fancier billboards advertised the likes of So & So Chest Pain Clinic and So & So Heartburn Redux Clinic.

Some of us in the Deep South subscribe to a life philosophy espoused by a pot-bellied pharmacist acquaintance: "Take acid-reflux pills, statin meds, and a fistful of fish oil pills every day and eat whatever you want."

These days, if that prescription doesn't carry the day and one runs into heart trouble, they have the perfect clinic. *Hey, hey, extra gravy for my country-fried steak, please.*

CATFISH

At a catfish restaurant, a stout gentleman at the neighboring table was praying feverishly over the fried bottom feeder on his plate until his phone buzzed. He stopped praying to return the text. First things first.

PEACH COBBLER

At a meat-and-three diner the other day, a rather large, big-boned couple strolled in and squeezed into the booth next to mine. The lady ordered her main course *and* peach cobbler. "Bring the cobbler out first, please."

The waitress did a stutter-step. "What? You want dessert first?"

"Yes," replied the patron. "I may get full and can't eat it all, and I want to make sure I eat that peach cobbler."

Many people talk the talk with slogans like, "Life is short, eat dessert first." Around these parts, we walk the walk.

SMALL-TOWN HOSPITAL

A divorced buddy was having outpatient surgery in a wee hospital in a small Georgia town. The poor son of a bitch had no interested party to be there for the procedure, so I stepped up. After the pre-op rigmarole and a brief talk with the surgeon, I said *adios* and they instructed me to wait by the telephone in the Outpatient Surgery Waiting Room, about ten whole paces away.

Caught up in a good novel, I looked forward to reading a chapter or two. As I entered the waiting room, a stooped octogenarian hovered in front of a blaring TV.

I settled into a seat by the phone and assessed the situation. The old man hung on every word of the newscast, even commercials. The volume was so loud, it was impossible to read my book. I needed earplugs or else I was going to be hard of hearing myself. This is typical US behavior—people so hooked on TV, they don't give a damn about imposing their extreme volume on everybody.

Unable to withstand it, I stood, approached the old geezer, and shouted, "SIR, CAN WE TURN IT DOWN?"

"WHAT?" he replied. "SORRY, I'M HARD OF HEAR-ING. I HAVE TO TURN IT UP OR I CAN'T HEAR IT."

I stumbled back to my seat, dazed by his answer. The rude old codger returned to total boob-tube absorption. Being "old" is no excuse for such behavior. I'm surprised he lived to be this old. Somebody should have taken him out by now. I contemplated it myself. Too bad I didn't bring my ax handle. Maybe grab a folding metal chair and bust him over the head, professional-wrasslin' style.

At the end of my rope, I wandered off to the little in-house cafeteria for a bite. A small lunch buffet featured two entrée choices: fried chicken or pulled pork. Three vegetable choices simmered beneath a fatty, ham-hock sheen. Want a salad? Take a tiny plastic plate, have some iceberg lettuce, shredded cheese, and high-fat dressing.

Hey, hospitals need to keep up business.

CORNHOLE

Back in the day, "cornhole" meant a few things, all related to the ass pipe. It could refer to anal sex, or "buggery" as we lawyers call it. Or, it could mean the bunghole itself. A noun or a verb, and an action verb at that.

Then, the now-popular lawn game exploded onto the scene, where players take turns throwing beanbags at a raised, slanted platform with a hole in the far end. Three points if it goes in the hole. One point if it stays on the platform. First to twenty-one wins. It's a nice little game. Problem is, some genius named it "cornhole." Really? So what, if you play with corn bags and the object is to land them in a hole, must you be oblivious to the *other* meanings of the word?

There is even an American Cornhole Association. Without researching, one would not know if that group consists of lawn game enthusiasts or anal sex jockeys. (It is the former.)

Before I knew about the name of the lawn game, a

friend telephoned. "Hey, come on over. A few of the boys and I are going to play cornhole in my backyard."

"What?" I said. "Are you crazy? I don't play that game."

"Come on, man. We've got beer. We'll take turns and switch partners. I know your back has been hurting, so we won't make you bend over very often."

"Not a chance, pal. I ain't no buttercup."

"Whatever, man. We're gonna play horseshoes next weekend. You wanna play?"

"You bet. I love lawn games."

COACHES' OUTFITS

In high school, baseball coaches wear the uniform of their team. The practice extends right up through the major league, where managers do the same.

I always loved to watch Tommy Lasorda, former manager of the Dodgers, waddle out to home plate in his uniform to give the umpire hell, his overlapping belly bouncing a jig.

If the practice is good enough for America's Pastime, it's good enough for other sports too. Let's have football coaches run up and down the sidelines in helmet and shoulder pads. Basketball coaches should pace in front of the bench in shorts to their knees and sleeveless jerseys. Ditto for hockey and right on down the line.

Forget business suits, khakis, polo shirts, sweatshirts, jackets, and the like. Grab a uniform. Come on, show team spirit and solidarity. Show some love.

LET'S CHAT

Used to be, "chat" meant two or more people speaking to one another face to face or by phone. Actually verbalizing words with their mouths in real time.

Nowadays, in the lingo of the times, "chat" means an online conversation. No talking involved. All on the keyboard. Social media, texting, email. Does anybody actually talk with anyone else these days? The art of being personable is slipping away.

As a species, our intelligence and incessant inventions often lead to sad, unintended consequences.

If you'd like to chat further about it, shoot me a text.

TAX DEDUCTIONS

HOME OFFICE

More and more folks these days work out of their homes, what with the internet, video conferencing, and all that. The tax code allows for the deduction of those home office expenses against income, but to do so requires a horrendous and onerous amount of bookkeeping. One must tally all of last year's expenditures on electricity, telephone, internet, cell phone, cable TV, garbage collection, pest control, propane, repairs and maintenance, and more.

My advice: Forget about the damn deduction. Don't bother. Running down the records and tallying the numbers is beyond what any non-geek, non-accountant citizen should endure.

I say pay the extra taxes. Forget the savings. You won't have as much money, but your brief time on Earth will now be less stressed and more dignified. I guarantee you will not achieve nirvana by gathering and tallying all those numbers. During those years when I claimed the home office deduction, the two most miserable times of year were gathering that tax return information and the digital rectal exam administered by my doctor, the man with the longest finger in the universe.

MILEAGE

For the mileage deduction on your personal car driven for business use, I'll make you aware of a different record-keeping tactic, a method used by a friend.

One is required to keep a log in one's car and record every business trip—the date, destination, purpose, and beginning and ending odometer reading.

"Oh, please," my friend argues, "do we not have better things to do? Screw keeping a log."

At tax prep time, he *estimates* his annual business mileage. CYA tip from him: "Make sure your stated beginning and end-of-year odometer readings don't conflict with your car's maintenance records."

If you receive an audit letter, he instructs, *then* you sit down and create that mileage log in one of those booklets they sell for that purpose. Another of his CYA tips: "Make sure the publication date of the booklet is prior to the year in audit. You wouldn't want to show up for a 2019 audit with a mileage log booklet published in 2020. Go ahead and purchase a few booklets now and you'll be set for future audits," he advises. "Failing that, you can always make your own log. You don't have to buy a preprinted booklet."

"To fill in the log," he continues, "you'll have to examine your calendar to remember the trips taken. Hop on the internet and get mileages from point A to point B. Write the information in the log with different-color pens, put a coffee mug stain on the cover, let Fido chew on it, handle it until brown finger stains etch certain spots and the pages grow dog-eared.

"In the *unlikely* event of an audit, you've handled the record-keeping in one sitting and avoided the indignity and humiliation of toting a damn booklet around all year, scribbling numbers like some trained monkey with nothing better to occupy your thoughts. *Let freedom ring.*"

So there you go, advice from one man.

To any IRS agents reading this, note that the "friend" referred to hereinabove is actually only an acquaintance, a distant one at that. He "was" an acquaintance, not "is." Been forever since I've seen him. Don't even remember his name. Yessir, I say everybody pay your taxes. IRS agents are our friends. They collect the money to build our bridges and defend our borders. Have you hugged *your* IRS agent today?

BE KIND TO TICKS

Ticks get a bad rap. All of God's creatures deserve respect. In Earth's grand ecological scheme, these ancient arthropods play an important role.

Ticks are an essential food source to reptiles, amphibians, and birds. Additionally, ticks host a variety of microorganisms that contribute to the ecological diversity of life. Finally, they help control the population of their larger hosts. Just ask the giraffe that died from housing fifty thousand of the bloodsuckers. Or the New Hampshire moose that accommodated ninety-five thousand. Research it if you think I'm lyin'.

Our bodies hold about twelve pints of blood. The tiny tick only wants a wee drop or two. So next time a tick has its head embedded in your skin, don't knee-jerk react and quickly yank out the poor thing. Don't be hatin' on ticks. Show some love. Let it feed for a few days. When it becomes too bloated, it will fall off.

Wouldn't that be a novel topic at a dinner party? You pull down your collar and point to the swollen tick on your neck. "Hey, guys, check this one out. Been with me for three days now."

"Oohs" and "ahhs" follow. "She's a beaut," they all concur.

"Check this one out," Rebecca announces as she stands, raises her blouse, and lowers the side of her bra. "Right on my titty. Four days now, I've been watching the little gal grow. She looks like a water balloon. Isn't she cute?"

Applause erupts. "Look," someone points out, "there's a bright-red rash circling the tick like it hit the bull's-eye."

"Yeah," Rebecca stammers, "I have a fever and my whole body aches something terrible."

"Don't complain, darling," the dinner host says, "we all know that every organism serves a purpose, and the tick is no exception. It's a small price we must pay for being part of an advanced and civilized society."

The host raises his wineglass: "Cheers to the lowly tick."

"Here, here," the refrain echoes.

"Let us all remember, July is National Adopt a Mosquito Month."

BUCK SNORTS

- ✓ When, why, and how did the pound (#) symbol become a "hashtag"?
- ✓ If you can't find it at Walmart Supercenter, you don't need it.
- ✓ I'm an author of rare books. I've written three that are unpublished.
- ✓ When forced by his spouse to complete the funeral home's "prearrangement form" before he was ready to deal with such weighty life matters, one good ole boy, under "church preference," wrote "red brick."
- ✓ At the golf course: "Y'all got room for one more?" "Sorry, we already have a threesome."

✓ I've been to Boston, Georgia, and Boston, Massachusetts. They have two noticeable similarities: 1) the names of the cities, and 2) their state's abbreviation—GA and MA—each end in "A."

EPA MINI-SUPERFUND SITES

We humans absorb mass amounts of poisons every year, but let's try not to stress over it. In fact, methinks we need to exercise our immune systems like muscles to keep them strong.

However, there is a limit to how much abuse our bodies can take. Therefore, I'm blowing the whistle on a hidden epidemic in this country.

In restaurants these days, before you take your seat, they spray your table with some chemical then wipe it "clean" with a rag or sponge harboring billions of serial bacteria. If you carry a microscope, you could see a chemical stew roiling on the table's surface. Accumulate enough of that crap, layer after layer, and you have an EPA mini-superfund site.

Staff expects you, the happy-go-lucky diner, to unwrap your eating utensils and plop them right on top of that superfund site.

No way, José. Don't play that game. Make 'em bring you another napkin on which to lay your nicked and battered "silverware."

Having saved myself from this form of restaurant

poisoning, I figure I can add one beer to my daily regimen. An even swap on the death-o-meter scale.

ONE BIG SCAM

From the very beginning of a child's life, we adults start weaving elaborate tales about Santa Claus, the Easter Bunny, the Tooth Fairy, and more. This is Phase I of a lifelong cycle of scamming.

One sad day, the truth dawns on every kid and we lapse into Phase II. It sinks into our psyches that our parents, the most trusted people in the universe, have hustled us with these massive frauds. In Phase II, kids can be downright snarky, as illustrated by the following note penned by one of my daughters and left on her pillow: "The tooth fairy is 5 day late—5$ late fee."

When we finally digest and process all those lies, we lapse into the permanent and final Phase III, the "pay it forward" stage, and embrace bullshitting as both science and art. Truth becomes too mundane and facts too boring for our voracious and nimble imaginations.

Those among us who really take it to heart become carnival hucksters, Ponzi schemers, or international double spies.

As an aside, Santa Claus has a semi-feasible mode of transportation with his sleigh and reindeer. But the Easter Bunny? Come on—he goes *hoppity-hop* bearing gifts to every child's house in the Christian world? One time, the Easter Bunny delivered an entire set of encyclopedias to my childhood friend. The Easter Bunny is loaded down enough with a basket for every child, but encyclopedias? Get outta town.

While we're at it—and I hate to burst your bubble on this—I have it on good authority that the reason Rudolph the Red-Nosed Reindeer's nose is so red and bright is due to chronic alcoholism. That's right, Rudolph's Siberian descent led to his voracious appetite for vodka, which produced that telltale sign of alcoholism—severe rosacea and rhinophyma, a.k.a. "drinker's nose." Think W. C. Fields, who, while alive, could have guided Santa's sleigh.

Back to Phase I of the scam. We drum into kids that, since Santa Claus is coming to town, they had better watch out, they had better not cry, better not pout . . .

What if some poor kid is playing outside and a field mouse bites him? He knows Santa won't visit if he cries or pouts. The kid sucks it up, doesn't tell his parents, contracts hantavirus, and dies. Are we happy now with this scam?

UTILITIES

Sadly, we've drifted away from the mantra that "the customer is always right." Now, simply put, it's more like "screw the customer."

Let me put it to you another way: utility companies don't give a rat's ass about you or me, my friends. It is us versus them.

A good example occurred recently when our TV satellite required tweaking. "Someone must be at the residence," the scheduler announced. "They must have access to the TV."

"Aw-right," I said. "What day?"

"Will Thursday work for you?" she asked. "Somewhere between eight a.m. and five p.m."

"What? Can't you narrow down the time?"

"Sorry, sir. That's our service policy."

Give me a break. That, *mis amigos*, is bullshit on steroids.

So I stay home all day waiting. Then, true story, they call about four thirty. "Sorry, the technician got detained and we'll have to reschedule."

This ever happen to you? No wonder heart attacks kill so many people in this country.

Here is another example of how utility companies have run amok: account numbers. How about this one: 74@0WbPHi615*%28996p/tFN#! My friends, computer geeks are running the world. At bill-pay time, instructions are always to write your account number on your check. That pisses me off. It would require mega sedative and a college degree in anger management to accurately reproduce the above permutation on your check.

If they wish for account numbers that *they* invented written on *our* checks, I say let *their* envelope-opening monkeys write them. Don't make us do it, for cryin' out loud. We have better things to do, don't we?

Okay, so the above account number was a bit of an embellishment. But the following is an honest-to-God account number assigned to me: 070000458262-0001. Am I going to attempt to write that number on my check? Hell no. Guess what—one number off and some schmuck in Peoria gets a strange credit on his account while I get a hostile letter from a collection goon and a black mark on my credit score.

While on the bill-pay topic, how about those invoice stubs that say, "Do not fold, staple, or paper-clip." This, once again, is for the convenience of the envelope-opening monkeys. I say if you want to send *me* a check, if it'll make you feel better, you can fold, staple, *and* paper-clip it.

Utilities all want us to "go paperless." They hide behind the "green friendly" banner, but it is, of course, to save *them* money. I'm old school and wish to have copies of certain records. If the statement is electronic only, I must print it on my dime. As is, they must print and mail it. Maybe I'm doing my share to help the US Postal Service stay afloat.

If utilities *really* want me to go paperless, they need to scratch the itch in my palm with some green. Show me the dough. Got to do better than some "go paperless" prize drawing where my name is put in the pot with ten million other customers to win a middling amount of money.

Undoubtedly, paper statements will soon be outdated. Even if you claim hardship, that you don't have a computer or smartphone, they will say, "Tough shit, mister, get your ass down to the public library."

Recently I received a rare admission of guilt from a utility. I wished to increase my internet speed and started my inquiry process with my internet provider's local sales office. The clerk said, "No can do." I refused to accept that answer and met with a service tech. He shook his head and said, "No can do." I climbed the ladder to his boss, a local engineer for the company, who said, "No can do." I climbed further up the chain and spoke with a regional engineer, a man who actually voiced common sense.

He looked at my address on his service grid, and said, "Sure, we can do it." I explained that three others before him said it couldn't be done. "You know," he said, "around here, sometimes, I feel like light in a sea of darkness."

Amen, brother, amen.

"Good customer service from a utility company"— oxymoron for the ages.

ANIMAL WHISPERER

DOG WHISPERER

I thought I was a dog whisperer until . . .

I'm getting ahead of myself. A little background first. I've always had a way with dogs and cats. We get along. I talk to them. I scratch the top of their heads and behind their ears and massage their temples, hitting all the right spots. We connect. I get it. I am a whisperer.

So I thought, until the day I went for a jog down a long country road.

Dogs, especially mean-spirited dogs, seem instinctively

suspicious of a human on the run. *You are a threat to my master*, they must think.

I had a good pace going, grooving to my tunes, when two crazed mongrels bolted from under a ramshackle singlewide trailer and dashed straight for me, barking to beat all hell. I commenced to whispering, as I've done a thousand times before.

It's okay, boy. Good dog. It's okay.

It was as if they didn't hear me a'tall. In the blink of an eye, one chomped my calf a good one. I hollered and blood gushed. Turns out, the dogs' owner hadn't gotten around to their rabies shots, which resulted in *my* taking the rabies series.

After replaying and processing the scene, I've concluded that these dogs simply didn't understand English.

Sidenote: Now that I've had the rabies shots, I'm not nearly as afraid of a frothing raccoon on the back porch during daylight hours as *you* should be.

FOX WHISPERER

A red fox occasionally darts around the woods behind my house. Today, the fox apparently didn't see me, as it trotted my way and stopped ten feet out.

Truly beautiful animals, this one sported black socks and a white-tipped bushy tail. After a few seconds, we made eye contact. I whispered, "It's okay, buddy."

It sprinted away. It apparently doesn't understand English either.

FUNHOUSE MIRROR

You need to know about the mirror mounted on the wall above the loo into which I whiz most often. I recommend that you, male or female, purchase one also.

It's a carnival mirror that distorts images vertically, making everything look long and tall. It's a great subliminal tool. I stand and stare at my three-foot manhood and afterward, I'm ready to conquer the universe. No task too large, no hurdle too high. Bring it on, sucker! Similar results can be achieved for mammary-challenged females.

INSURANCE

ANNUITY

Have you ever examined the financial statements of giant life insurance companies? Their enormous incomes exceed the GDP of most countries, literally. So, if you're planning your affairs with help from one of these outfits, which should you purchase, a life insurance policy or a lifetime annuity?

With life insurance, the insurance company wants you to live. With an annuity, they want you to die. I can envision one of these companies falling short of income expectations, so word comes down to terminate some annuity holders.

Pass on the annuity, thank you, and take life insurance.

TERM POLICY

So I met with an overcaffeinated salesman and he produced several papers with differing policy offerings. He wrote, drew, and highlighted all over the term sheets like a football coach drawing up three plays simultaneously on the whiteboard.

I pulled the trigger on a plan just to get the guy out of my office. Days later, I looked at the papers and had no clue what most of his markings meant. Circles, underlines, arrows, exclamation points, yellow and purple everywhere, as though an engineer illustrated the launch and trajectory of a rocket. What did his directionals mean? They prove he expounded loquaciously, and I can never claim he didn't.

Yes, I have a term life insurance policy. You may be thinking my wife has incentive to knock me off so she can get the cash. Quite the contrary.

Under the law, if she is caught hastening my demise, she gets zero from the policy. Her best bet is to pass on murder and hope I perish by means not of her doing. Apparently, she realizes this, as she encourages me to climb tall ladders and constantly sends me to the grocery store during the coronavirus pandemic.

After the policy expires, her *disincentive* to kill me goes away. Are you thinking what I'm thinking? I believe I'll keep that policy in force.

Update: The premiums under the aforementioned term policy were level for several years. The new premium was stratospheric, so I let it lapse.

As its expiration date neared, it bugged me that on paper, I was worth more dead than alive. Then, when it lapsed, at midnight I was instantaneously worth more alive than dead.

Problem is, my wife's insurance-driven homicide disincentive is now gone and she polishes her kitchen knives with a gleam in her eye. Maybe I should have life insurance after all to help *ensure* that I stay alive.

HOME/AUTO

You dutifully pay your premiums year in and year out. Then, you have a small claim. Your agent says, "Oh, you don't want to file *that* claim. They will only raise your premium."

The greedy bastards should welcome small claims and be thankful that they are not large claims.

BBC

You can tune into BBC International if you want to discover what's happening outside our insular US microcosm. They once reported, incorrectly, on a snowstorm here in the States.

The weather woman pointed to areas shaded in pink on the US map and explained in her formal British accent, "Parts of the Northeast are being hit with up to fifty centimeters of snow."

What? Did she say centimeters? Does BBC not realize we've not adopted the metric system on this side of the pond? It doesn't snow in centimeters over here, it snows in *inches.*

"Temperatures have dipped to minus twenty degrees Celsius," she continued.

Wrong, wrong, wrong. Temperatures over here don't comprehend Celsius. They only know Fahrenheit. That's as wrong as me going to my local Walmart deli and asking for half a kilogram of sliced turkey. Good luck with that.

NATURAL DISASTERS

Who are the bigger gamblers in the US—East or West Coast dwellers? East Coasters gamble with hurricanes; West Coasters with earthquakes.

What's the big deal about living in an active earthquake zone? When one hits, just dance a little two-step to keep your balance, right?

Seems like the ever-looming possibility of a quake—the Big One—would add an element of mystery and danger to one's life. With hurricanes nowadays, we know well in advance. How boring.

There are some distinct disadvantages to not knowing when an earthquake may strike. Let's say you're working a posh soirée, talented and capable of carrying high the tray of crystal champagne-laden flutes balanced on five fingertips as you dance around the hall distributing your wares. But no, because the Big One could hit any moment, the boss instructs you to hold the tray with both hands at waist level so when the building does shimmy and shake, the flutes won't go a-flyin'. How boring.

Or, you're in a San Francisco operating room performing brain surgery when it strikes—*oops*, you whisper as a frontal lobe splashes the floor.

On the East Coast, a cottage industry has emerged, designed to whip the populace into a frenzy when a one-eyed, swirling grim reaper lurks in the Atlantic. The Weather Channel and others hope for brutal hurricane seasons, so consumers chain themselves to round-the-clock coverage.

Idiot correspondents hopped up on bravado and yelling frantic histrionics into mikes charge right in and hug telephone poles as hurricane-force winds horizontally levitate their bodies. Why? Sensationalize in order to achieve better ratings so they can raise prices on advertising spots, the cost of which is being passed on to you and me, Mr. and Ms. Average Consumer. *Cha-ching.*

I keep waiting for a tree limb to impale a reporter's chest on live TV. Maybe then they'll stop hamming it up. Or how about a roof shingle decapitation? Maybe blunt-force instant death from a collision with a flying cow. You get my drift. This possibility of a reporter fatality helps drive ratings, which only encourages more hype. I'm afraid there is no turning back.

Dire hurricane warnings days in advance send cars pouring out of Florida like rats off a sinking ship, clogging Georgia roadways. During a mass evacuation a few seasons back, I faced the option of staying home or parking on the highway for a few days with my million closest friends from the Sunshine State. (I rode it out at home.)

A monster hurricane (redundant) recently barreled toward Georgia's coastline, targeting Socrates's hometown. He phoned and I immediately sensed his agitation.

"You know we lie in the 'cone of uncertainty.'"

"Of course I know. I've been glued to the TV."

"I'm in a serious situation right now." His voice sounded shaky.

"What's that?"

"I'm walking into Dairy Queen and don't know if I want chocolate, vanilla, or strawberry—it's a cone of uncertainty. Now I'm in a DOUBLE cone of uncertainty. What should I do?"

I coached him through some breathing techniques. "Just buy chocolate and tick one cone of uncertainty off your list. More importantly, you had better go stock up on beer and ice before they sell out."

Socrates phoned later that evening, confirming that he had scored beer and ice, and relaying a conversation he overheard while gassing up his truck.

A car pulled up to the adjoining pump and a woman and boy emerged.

"Here," she said, handing the boy some money, "go pay for ten dollars' worth o' gas."

"But Mama, we only buy five dollars at a time."

"You idiot! Don't you know a storm's comin'!"

In the midst of it all, the East and West Coast construction beat goes on. Crapshooters all. So you decide—who are the bigger gamblers?

LET 'EM TOUGH IT OUT

It pisses me off that every time a hurricane hits one of our coastlines, the federal government rushes in to bail out folks in trouble by using money taken from the rest of us.

People live along seashores because of the ambiance of the ocean and its healing effects, physical and mental.

But these people are taking a known risk by dwelling oceanside. The rest of us, being more prudent and risk-averse, settle for life without. Yet, when disaster strikes, we landlubbers are forced to pony up to subsidize those seaside. It ain't right.

It's time to cut the umbilical cord, to say bugger off to the coast dwellers. No more federally subsidized flood insurance. Let the free market set the premiums. No more mass giveaways every time a hurricane strikes. Let 'em fend for themselves, since they knew disaster was inevitable.

One's choice of domicile should be risk/reward behavior. But no, says our federal government, lets spread the oceanfront risk, even to us schmucks who look out our windows and see not the beautiful sea, but tumbleweeds rolling across the barren landscape.

Fellow landlubbers, it's time we called bullshit on this one.

YOU KNOW YOU'RE DRIVING DRUNK WHEN . . .

. . . you flip on your car's blinker in your own driveway because there is a slight veer to the left. There are no other cars in sight. You realize your foolishness and accidentally hit the emergency flasher as you try to silence the blinker. Then you fiddle to turn off the flashers, and next you know, *BAM*, you slam into the garage door. *Oops, forgot to push that button.* Then you glance down at your bare feet working the pedals and wonder what the hell happened to your shoes.

Now I know how Cinderella felt when she lost her slipper. Rhetorical question: How does one lose her shoe at midnight if alcohol is not involved? Could the punch bowl at the ball have been spiked?

SHERIFF'S RANCH

Speaking of driving when you shouldn't, here's a tip: it's money well spent to support your state's Sheriffs' Association, or whatever it's called in your area. Be sure to get one of those rear-window decals displaying a badge. Hey, if the decal wins you the benefit of the doubt just once, it is worth a lifetime of annual twenty-dollar donations.

The drawback is you must be mindful of where you travel. Parking in the wrong section of town may likely gain you a smashed windshield, or worse.

Update: "Back the Blue" stickers and decals are now popular to show support for law enforcement. The image is simple and classic—black with a thin blue line. Purchase just one and you don't have to pay annually to keep it current. (See, sometimes us average janes and joes catch a break.)

Another alternative: Some states now offer "Back the Blue" automobile license plates. It'll cost you a few nickels every year, but actual dollars flow to actual police causes. That should put them in a forgiving, warning-ticket-only mode when they pull you over.

CASSEROLE CONUNDRUM

Hey guys, your woman ever cooked an awful-tasting casserole? How does one handle that situation?

My wife is a great cook. Excuse me—a great *chef*. But occasionally she runs across a bad recipe, that's all.

Happened just the other day. She didn't have a couple of the recipe's ingredients, so she substituted. "All chefs improvise from time to time—even Julia," she waxed eloquent in Julia's soprano voice as she waved her hand in the air.

Foreign ingredients must have triggered some feral chemical reaction in the cauldron. I took one bite and fought to restrain my knee-jerk reaction to grab the cat and lick its ass to get the taste out of my mouth. (You may be thinking this is sheer embellishment, but no, I'm being quite literal.)

"So, what do you think?" she said, sitting on the edge of her chair, leaning forward, eyebrows raised.

"A-hum," I cleared my throat, fighting back a gag. "It's good."

What was I supposed to say, keeping in mind that she is sensitive and delicate about her chefery and is the type who requires positive reinforcement?

"Oh, wonderful," she said. "Thank you. I needed to hear that."

Of course, you know what happens when you praise a culinary creation.

First, I had to scrub the glass dish, and scrub like hell I did because that crap was seared on as if the Pyrex and the voodoo casserole had become one.

Worse yet, that casserole is now part of the menu rotation. Because of the kumbaya atmosphere I strive to maintain, these types of conundrums haunt my exist-ence.

AT THE MOVIES

The big-screen movie theater has always been a place where one can gain temporary relief from the rampant commercialism through which one must suffer while watching TV.

Because there are few things in life I loathe more than

missing the beginning of a movie, I usually arrive plenty early. I expect to see a half-dozen movie previews. These days, however, before the previews, they run commercial after commercial, many of them the same damn ones we suffer through on TV. That really pisses me off.

So much for that formerly commercial-free zone. Thanks, movie people, you horny-palmed sons o' bitches.

Before the show begins, the big screen instructs you to deposit your litter in the trash cans at the exits. I call bullshit. A soft drink, popcorn, and a box of chocolates will set you back about a month's rent on a singlewide. I say tuxedo-clad attendants should sweep up after every movie and thank us for the opportunity to be of service.

Hell, for what they charge for refreshments, white-gloved attendants should be stationed at the urinals to service us after we whiz, to shake our peckers and wipe their noses with a hanky.

GONE TO POT

Sometimes you'll go into a dining establishment and the server will tell you about the "salmon" special. She'll pronounce salmon by enunciating the "l" like this: săl' mən. As opposed to the proper way where the "l" is silent: săm' ən.

I can let it slide coming from a waitress in a hamburger joint. But the other day, I was in a seafood restaurant and damned if the waitress didn't do the same thing. "How would you like your săl' mən prepared?" Come on, for cryin' out loud, a seafood joint? This country has gone to pot.

A REAL PLAYA'

I worked with a fellow who was quite the lady-killer. This guy knew how to talk the talk. His bold approach often resulted in a slap in the face, or sometimes, in his getting laid.

More than once, we'd step onto an elevator and there was a babe on board. Didn't matter if we were heading up or down, he'd look the gal in the eye, wink, and with a sly grin, say, "Are you going down?"

I called him on the carpet one day. Told him he was a chauvinist, predator, and pervert.

"Hey, I'm no chauvinist, pal," he said. "Just because I subscribe to the theory that all women, turned upside down, look alike, doesn't mean I don't respect women. Come on, gimme a break."

Believe me, friends, I am as offended by that insensitive remark as you. As an investigative journalist, I report the comment to provide a glimpse of the depravity out there. Shows we need more sensitivity training.

Hey—now there's something I could teach.

LOVE DOCTOR

Roger was a young, single man I'd known since he was a boy. He skipped college and landed a job in an office of about a hundred workers, mostly women. His comments led me to believe that he was growing more cognizant of the subtle beauty of the fairer sex. But he was inexperienced and clumsy around the ladies. They were a mystery to him. (I didn't have the heart to tell him the riddle only grows more complex with time.)

He asked me how to break the ice with the babes. I donned my Love Doctor thinking cap and devised a plan. We typed and printed a note:

> Dear Roger, my wild lover.
>
> Thanks for the roses. You are such a romantic and stud. You were spectacular the other night. Gives me chill bumps to think about it! Can we please get together again soon?!?!
>
> Love, XOXO

He arrived early for work the next morning, made multiple copies of the note, and strategically placed them in the copy room, the ladies' room, and the break room. To avoid suspicion, he then went for a Starbucks coffee and arrived fifteen minutes late.

Women in the office quickly warmed up to him. He got dates, got laid, and lived happily ever after.

The Doctor of L♥ve at your service.

TALK THE TALK

When it comes to sex, young boys learn to talk the talk long before they are capable of walking the walk. How do they learn the talk? Word gets around. Older ones love to shock youngsters with mysterious and curious details of sex.

Cooter grew up in a small town and tells of an incident when he was ten years old. A group of boys would stroll the Main Street sidewalk after school. One day, like most days, the all-knowing old ones with their knobby, liver-spotted hands were rocking in their chairs outside the feed-and-seed store discussing the plight of the world.

"Hey, what are y'all talking about?" Cooter asked.

"Oral sex," came the reply.

"What is that?"

There followed a detailed explanation from the wise ones. The young boys were stunned, never heard anything like it. Unbeknownst to them, just like that, they learned of a major driving ambition for their upcoming adult lives.

Then, one of the geezers giggled and said, "If you really want a *good* blow job, get a woman to do it," whereupon the wise ones cackled and wheezed with laughter.

In the summer after ninth grade, a buddy and I worked at a resort restaurant. Many times, young girls our age dined with their parents. We'd be out there bussing tables, pouring water, and making every crazy excuse to mingle around the prettiest girl.

Back in the kitchen: "Man, I'd like to have a go at that."

"Yeah, I'd make her cry for her mama."

"I'd wear that thing out."

Spoken by wise virgins armed with vague notions about topics like some mysterious little man in a boat, we had no idea how to actually walk the walk, but that didn't stop us from talking the talk.

NATIONAL CHAMPIONSHIP

The NCAA football season is finally concluding. The big National Championship game is tonight. Did I bet on the right team? The hype and anticipation overtake me. I commence drinking beer too early for a game that will not end until after midnight and am well into brown liquor by game time.

At halftime, I slide to horizontal on the couch. I've overcooked it. My head starts spinning. I rub my forehead and temple, trying not to throw up, not to blow my cookies. I inch one foot to the floor, to drop anchor, to steady the ship.

There's too much sensory input, so I mute the TV. The screen's flashing light nauseates me, so I turn it off. I avoid watching the swirling ceiling fan blades that would surely make me hurl; just listening to them shoves me to the brink. I study the fissured-texture ceiling tiles through squinted eyelids. *How do they make those things?*

Next I know, it's 2:00 a.m. I stumble to bed. Before passing out, I whip out my smartphone to check the score. *Yes, I won.* I conk out with a throbbing head and a smile on my face. Hell of a way to end the season.

ADDICTIONS

My wife was gracious enough to recently enumerate my three worst addictions. "You have an issue with each one," she stressed.

I relayed my berating to Socrates.

"Oh no," he pontificated, "three is an optimum number. With three, you can spread it out. It's the people who have only one main addiction who get their ass into a bind."

BUCKET LIST

Socrates built houses for part of his career. He told me the following story:

"Cecil, the painter, was bad to play games. His favorite was to write 'SHRIMP' on the top of a sheetrock bucket. Then, he'd shit into the bucket a couple of times and build up a nice pile.

"When a new man would appear on the job site, Cecil would warm up to the guy, and then say, 'Hey, I pulled my shrimp net yesterday and caught a bunch. I'm givin' 'em away. Would you like some?'

"'Of course.'

"So Cecil would walk the guy toward the bucket and point. 'There you go. Help yourself.'

"Naturally, the fellow would open the bucket to take a look at the shrimp."

Oh my. Welcome to Cecil's world.

I relayed this story to the young man who is painting

our house. "Oh yeah," he said, "painters are the worst. On one job, my boss left behind a little surprise for the cleanup crew. He shit into a sheetrock bucket and left it. I was doing some touch-up work when the cleanup crew came across it. Naturally, they opened the bucket to see what was inside. Let me tell you, you coulda heard that clean-up gal holler all the way to the moon.

"Another thing—if a painter is pissed at the owner, I've seen 'em shit in hidden places, leave a little surprise."

Moral: Gotta keep an eye on those painters.

What's in your bucket?

CONDO NAZIS

Needing a getaway, we rented a condo on the South Carolina beach. I lugged our bags up the stairs, grabbed my first beer of the day, and settled into an easy chair to take in the ocean view.

I scooped up the dreaded black binder of compulsory rules and regulations.

DON'T DO THIS! DON'T DO THAT!! MAKE SURE TO DO THIS!! IT'S IMPERATIVE YOU DON'T DO THIS!!! On and on it went. The over-caffeinated Condo Nazis were working under the emphatic assumption that all we renters, poor schmucks like me paying the bills, are raving fools and babbling idiots. Their overarching goal, of course, is to make things easier on themselves.

Additional admonitions and rebukes were posted with military precision in every room and hallway. Apparently, every indiscretion by every prior occupant was represented by a "DO NOT!" sign.

- DO NOT LEAVE THE SLIDING DOOR OPEN AND THE AC RUNNING!
- DO NOT LEAVE THE DOOR TO THE REFRIGERATOR OR FREEZER OPEN!
- DO NOT SWING FROM CHANDELIER!

And so on, ad nauseam. These Condo Nazis never took a break.

Exhausted from reading their rules, and certain that I was violating one with my every move, I said to my wife, "Screw this. Don't even unpack. We're driving home in the morning to get some rest."

BAD DAY

You know you are having a bad day when 1) your wife is pissed at you all day for no reasonable reason, 2) you lose your NBA bet by half a point (fourteen stinking missed free throws), and 3) your dog nips your hand as you pet her on the way to bed, something she has never done. Time to give up the ghost.

HAZY DAYS

For several decades, I've noticed something is "off" with me. The symptoms vary from foot-in-mouth disease to an abnormal worldview. A self-evaluation and diagnosis seeking clues to the root of the malady reveal multiple candidates.

Some date back to my youth in the 1960s when the world was blissfully ignorant of many dangers like cigarette smoking, skin cancer, and chemical exposure.

A few times in the summer, my parents loaded the kids into the station wagon and we drove to the beach on the Gulf of Mexico. At the shoreline, large, overhead pipes supported by metal stanchions extended a hundred yards or so into the water through which raw sewage flowed. (Modern-day real estate developers, eat your heart out.)

On outgoing tides, we played in the Gulf. But on incoming tides, orders came down to play on the beach. So what if we kids suffered a bit of nausea, diarrhea, fever, and malaise—we had a swell time.

In our subdivision, periodically a mosquito truck slowly rolled down the streets, blowing a dense cloud of poison behind it. We kids made a big game out of it, following the truck and dashing into its fog, jogging from block to block, seeing who could disappear in the mist the longest.

The average human brain contains about a hundred billion cells. I figure I fried several billion in those E. coli beach–bathing, mosquito fog–chasing days. And that was before I started drinking. But that's okay. If all brain cells remained intact, my thoughts would probably run along the lines of $E = mc^2$, Einstein's nuclear fusion equation, or the classic binomial theorem $(x + a)^n = \sum_{k=0}^{n} \binom{n}{k} x^k a^{n-k}$. I don't have time for all that nonsense.

MUG SHOT ADVICE

Prudent people plan. Don't wait until your (next) arrest to practice your mug shot in front of the mirror. Mug shots are public record, you know, and may pop up anywhere, anytime, so you don't want to convey the wrong message.

What is your message? Angry? Frightened? Sad? Happy?

Anger is understandable. *Damn, this was not supposed to happen.*

Frightened is notable, especially if you'll be spending time in the pokey. *Pucker up, sweet cheeks.*

Sad? Maybe, but you don't want to appear guilty.

Happy? No way. Next thing you know, they'll transfer you to the nervous hospital.

I recommend a slight smile (*I'm innocent and will beat these bogus charges*), but with concerned eyebrows (*Yeah, I'll win, but it's gonna be a pain in the ass*). Look directly and confidently at the camera lens (*I know exactly what's happening here and I've got the situation under control*).

Of course, all this assumes that you are sober and cognizant enough to 1) remember this advice, and 2) control your facial expressions.

So, to the miscreants among us, get in front of that mirror and practice, practice, practice.

WORMS

If reincarnation is real, I wouldn't want to come back as a worm.

Today I fished the old-fashioned way—with worms. The earthy tubes of dirt-meat slept in their little plastic cup when I bought them, all balled up and wound one around another, in a stupor, living in a wad of castings—mud wet from their own excretions. I opened the lid and touched one. It barely moved. Alive is the best one can expect under those circumstances.

They are such cute, affectionate creatures. In preparing to put them to work, you pull one out of the cup and lay it in your palm. It makes slow-moving love to your hand, tickling your palm, thrilled to be out of that hellhole.

Then you start giving your sleepy little friend the big stick with the fishhook and suddenly it goes berserk, squirming to beat all hell. You thread the hook in several places, disemboweling it in the process. It's still squirming as it disappears into the water to await its denouement.

Anyone who thinks that worms and other invertebrates possess no physical feelings, gore one with a hook and you shall see.

The way of the fishing worm is not the way I wish to meet my maker. Maybe I can reincarnate as my dog, Molly. That's the ticket.

SPHINCTER APPRECIATION DAY

There is good reason why that set of muscles forming a ring around your anal canal is the most important muscle group in your body. Your sphincter muscles are the gatekeeper of your underdrawers and your dignity, on call 24/7. It is crucial for them to discern between gas and "other," which they skillfully do (if working properly), even when you sleep. A wrong decision by them and you're in deep . . .

For this reason, I have asked my congressman to sponsor a bill creating Sphincter Appreciation Day as a new national holiday. There will be parades in every city, speeches on the steps of City Hall, fireworks, apple pie, you name it. This will be big. Tremendous. Trust me on this.

Sphincter-shaped floats will pulse down the parade route, its riders tossing rubber sphincters to frenzied crowds. Fashionable women will convert them into bracelets and earrings. The Sphincter Ring Toss will become an Olympic sport.

Recognition needs to flow where recognition is due.

This is not to suggest by any means that sphincters nationwide will get a day off. Oh, heavens no. To the contrary, on Sphincter Appreciation Day, we should gorge on chili dogs and milkshakes. Make the sphincters work double time. All muscles need exercise. An active sphincter is a happy sphincter.

UNDER OATH

If you lie when you are "under oath," when you've sworn by the court to tell the truth, you commit a crime.

But should we not always conduct ourselves as if we're under oath? If we state a fact, shouldn't we have the integrity to self-impose an oath?

We're lucky that recreational lying is no crime. If it were, we'd all be in jail. Everyone, that is, except George Washington and me. We have never lied.

WIGGLING EARS

Molly's wagging tail is a surefire indicator that she's happy. Wouldn't it be nice if humans had a similar feature that reveals when they are lying? Maybe our ears should wiggle.

The Wiggling Ear Lie Detector Test might prompt crafty politicians to grow their hair long to hide their ears. Preventative laws would have to be enacted. Maybe amend the US Constitution for the twenty-eighth time: "No person in the United States, whether here legally or illegally, may obscure, in any form or fashion, a clear view of their ears."

Then politicians, used car salespersons, and other miscellaneous circus-barker types, drawn to loopholes like moths to a flame, would start amputating their ears. The Twenty-Eighth Amendment will need to be a living, breathing edict to cover all future attempts to evade its original intent.

A MANEUVER

At a restaurant today, a poster illustrating the Heimlich maneuver hung on the restroom wall. I got to thinking about Dr. Heimlich, and that a "maneuver" bears his name. How cool would that be, having a maneuver named after you?

Therefore, I've devised my own maneuver—Jameson's Double Texas Pile Driver. We all know the Texas Pile Driver move, right? In professional wrestling, Wrestler A clamps a standing headlock on Wrestler B. They charge in lockstep across the ring, leap in unison, and Wrestler A slams, or "pile-drives," Wrestler B's head into the canvas.

After a well-executed Texas Pile Driver, an uncontested three-count pin over the semiconscious victim inevitably follows. Match over.

With Jameson's Double Texas Pile Driver maneuver, Wrestler A clamps a headlock on Wrestlers B *and* C, one under each arm. He slams their heads together for a nice *CRACK*, then simultaneously pile-drives their now-limp bodies into the canvas.

Please know that my maneuver is not limited to professional wrestling inside the "squared circle." It can come in handy anytime hostile combatants outnumber you. I've personally tested my maneuver on twin midgets who live down the street and can guarantee its effectiveness.

It is a maneuver, my friends, to which I lend my name with honor. Dr. Heimlich and I, two peas in a pod, cut from the same cloth, birds of a feather, compadres of innovation singularly focused on improving the plight of humankind.

INTERSTATE FUN

I'd love to be a traffic engineer for a day.

I'd locate an exit-only lane on the interstate and remove all warning signs indicating such. Just before the exit, there would be a small flashing sign: NO RETURN ACCESS.

Then I'd set up a lawn chair at the edge of the woods, eat popcorn, drink beer, and watch cars and trucks crash and pile up at 80 mph.

Tell me that wouldn't be fun!

BLUE MIND EFFECT

Those of us not privileged to live beside water miss out on that personal and emotional relationship our bodies and minds have with water. We feel more relaxed and meditative when we are near water, where we can forget the stress and focus on the calm, a state known as "Blue Mind" effect.

For those not so privileged, here's what you can do to achieve your own Blue Mind effect:

Find a good pot suitable for boiling water, the bigger the better. An outdoor pit and an iron pot are best, but stovetop will work. Pull up chairs, stools, whatever lets you view the water inside the pot, and commence the boil.

It takes forever for anything to happen, and you'll think

"a watched pot never boils" is true. Then little swirls form in the water, followed by tiny whirls of rising steam. Next come little bubbles, five, ten, then too many to count. Next you know, you've got a full boil.

Mesmerizing. Of course, it'd probably help if you dropped acid prior to.

BIPOLAR

Why is being "bipolar" such a big deal these days? It's all the rage in the psych community.

We need to get over it. We have been bipolar since the dawn of our species and will remain so. That's how we are wired. We all have mood swings, ups and downs, good days and bad days. We all ebb and flow, wax and wane, zig and zag. There will always be night and day, flux and reflux, back and forth, to and fro, tick and tack, yin and yang. Even Earth is bipolar.

You don't need a prescription for that. Maybe there is the occasional exception, but not for half the damn folks out there? Come on, people.

BUCK SNORTS

- ✓ Isn't "emergency appendectomy" redundant? Does anybody ever have an elective appendectomy?
- ✓ Simple carbs is my favorite food group.
- ✓ Why do we still have hair in our armpits? So it won't

get cold under there? I don't think so; it's plenty warm and cozy. Can the human evolution process hurry up already and eliminate the underarm beard?

✓ Ever bite the inside of your cheek while eating? It swells, causing you to bite it again. It swells more, causing you to bite it yet again. It swells more . . . sometimes life is a bitch, ain't it?

✓ Beer and pork ribs go together like peas and carrots, but hold the vegetables, please, and pass the statins, nitroglycerin, and Gas-X.

✓ Have you noticed that you don't see many black kids these days named Jake or Sophia, and not many white kids named DeShawn or Ebony, nor many Latinos named Bjørn or Olga?

✓ The lady working at the health food store today was easily sixty pounds overweight. What does that tell you? "Yeah, sugar babe, give me some of what you're takin'."

BOXERS

I love boxer undershorts and the open flap in front. I wear them backward so when I need to "drop the kids off at the pool," I only need to lower my trousers; no need to drop my drawers. Just vamoose the kids through the flap. Saves a lot of time. I'm a busy guy.

If they would make underbritches with a flap in front *and* back, we'd be golden.

PEEPER

Topeka, Kansas (AP) — An unnamed prominent member of the community was recently arrested and charged with multiple counts of "Peeping Tom."

Sources reveal that over a private lunch, the gentleman explained to the judge that the ole gal had really big tits.

The judge, being a titty man himself, quashed the charges over the objection of the DA, who is an ass man.

A NON-EVENT

I have scheduled a live Facebook non-event for Tuesday of next week beginning at 11:16 a.m. For ten minutes, I will sit perfectly still and stare at a blank spot on the wall. Please remember to "like" it.

ESSAYS

THE GREATEST
ATHLETE OF OUR TIME

NOTES FROM A GAMBLER'S DIARY

July 4, 2017

Who do you think is the Greatest Athlete of Our Time? What sport does that person play? Football, basketball, baseball? Track and field, hockey, golf?

None of the above, actually. Fairness and logic dictate that the Greatest Athlete comes from our greatest national pastime—gluttony.

If you don't believe that feasting is our nation's greatest passion, take notice next time you stroll around at a superstore. I'm not casting stones, mind you, for I am no featherweight.

So if eating is our true pastime, the greatest eater must be the Greatest Athlete, and that, my friends, would easily be California's Joey "Jaws" Chestnut, competitive eating juggernaut. As of this morning, Jaws is ranked first in the world by Major League Eating. Last year he won his ninth World Championship of Competitive Eating crown at the annual July Fourth Nathan's Hot Dog Eating Contest on Coney Island, New York.

Today, he is gunning for his tenth World Championship. Allow me to repeat—World Champion ten times.

Imagine one quarterback winning the Super Bowl ten times. Or one golfer winning the Masters ten times. They would be super athletes and superheroes, indeed, but none would have achieved those feats in our nation's largest participation sport. None, that is, save Joey Chestnut.

If athletes like LeBron or Brady, Woods or Gretzky, thought they stood a chance against Jaws, do you think they would compete in Nathan's Hot Dog Eating Contest, the sporting world's ultimate prize? Hell yeah, they would.

In addition to Joey's nine World Championships, he currently holds forty-three world records in forty-three disciplines, including Twinkies (121 in six minutes), chicken wings (188 in twelve minutes), chili (two and a half gallons in six minutes), and hard-boiled eggs (141 in eight minutes). Any of those other guys hold forty-three world records at once? I think not.

Joey also holds the apple pie world record, having gulped 4.375 three-pound pies in eight minutes, providing literal meaning to the phrase "stuffing your pie hole."

Nathan's Hot Dog Eating Contest, a brilliant concept indeed—the only thing more American than eating hot dogs on Independence Day is eating them competitively. The Nathan's people claim their first contest was in 1916, but recorded results on their website go back only to 1972. (The history of eating in great haste goes back to pre-Neanderthals. Often when they killed a goat, they'd have only ten minutes to eat their fill before Tyrannosaurus rex came crashing down upon their asses.)

The annual contest to see who can scarf the most

Nathan's Famous hot dogs and buns (HDB) in short order rocked along for years, with the record slowly inching from the teens to the midtwenties. Then along came Japan's Takeru "Tsunami" Kobayashi who shocked the world at the 2001 Nathan's contest by downing fifty.

Like his namesake, he unleashed a tsunami on the sport, elevating it to stunning new heights and changing it forever. A disruptive influence for sure. One small step for man, one giant step for mankind.

Tsunami was a rock star and King of the Hill for several years, winning Nathan's six years running, until the arrival of Joey Chestnut, America's hero. Joey bested Tsunami in 2007 and continued his wiener-winning ways by crushing the competition eight years in a row.

After Joey's 2007 victory, Tsunami nipped at his heels for several years, challenging, always the bridesmaid, never the bride. He faded from the scene, due in part to contract disputes with Major League Eating.

Enter a new challenger to Joey's throne, Matt "Megatoad" Stonie. Megatoad is American of Japanese descent. There have been many Japanese superstar eaters and one should never underestimate them in an eating contest. They are ferocious eaters and take the sport very seriously.

As the record inched higher over the years, Joey kept pushing the limits of human skill and endurance. In 2012, after scarfing sixty-eight at Nathan's, he proclaimed that he "will not stop until I reach seventy," a boast and promise equally as bold as JFK's proclamation in 1962, to wit: "We choose to go to the moon in this decade, not because it is easy, but because it is h-a-a-r-d."

Megatoad finished second to Joey at Nathan's in 2013 and 2014. Then, in one of the biggest upsets in sports history, the Toad beat Joey in 2015 by downing sixty-two to Joey's sixty. Joey was not on his game that day.

The sporting world thought Joey was fading after his loss to Megatoad, but how wrong they were. Jaws was pissed. The very next year, 2016, he regained the Mustard Belt by downing seventy to the Toad's fifty-three. That's an ass-whoopin', folks.

Joey had finally reached his audacious goal of seventy, a feat akin to Roger Bannister running the first sub-four-minute mile in 1954, and Usain "Lightning" Bolt's unprecedented "triple-triple," when he sprinted to victory in the 100, 200, and 4x100 meter races at the 2008, 2012, and 2016 Olympics.

As the big 2017 contest approached, I decided to lay a bet to make it *really* exciting. Wagering cash on sporting events has been a tradition dating back to the Phoenicians' invention of money. Since we are all products of our past, why fight it? I stepped up to the plate.

Vegas set Joey's odds of winning at –450 (risk $450 to win $100). Heavily favored, yes, but not prohibitively so due to Megatoad's record. Coming in, the Toad was looking strong, having recently set world records for MoonPies (85 in eight minutes) and Peeps (255 in five minutes). Obviously, the man has talent.

Joey was not exactly chopped liver entering the contest.

In his training, he set world records in shrimp cocktail (fifteen pounds in eight minutes), glazed donuts (fifty-five in eight minutes), and ice cream sandwiches (twenty-five in six minutes). (Note to self: You could challenge for the ice cream sandwich record and would have a swell time training.)

A problem I have with laying short odds on a competitive eater is the vomit factor. If one hurls during a contest, one is disqualified. (That danger, by the way, is why they station a bucket at the feet of each contestant.) Though I never heard of Joey puking during a contest, I imagine it can happen to the best of them.

The other wagering option was even money (plus 10 percent juice on a loss) on the over/under, which was set at 71.5 HDB. That is a crazy high number. In his previous three wins at Nathan's, Joey downed 60, 61, and 70. What if Joey's body rebels against him, even just for a moment? Or he just isn't on top of his game that day? What if it's an extra hot and humid day?

Nevertheless, smart money always bets on a true champion. Joey trains like a warrior all year then fasts for two-to-three days before the big event. I knew I could count on him, so I took the OVER. Joey would have to down seventy-one and a half in ten minutes for a tie, seventy-two for a win.

As the contestants on Coney Island prepped backstage, kids scurried around our backyard throwing footballs and detonating firecrackers. Men hovered around the grill while women faffed about in the kitchen, all timed for a feast to coincide with ESPN's coverage of Nathan's World Championship of Competitive Eating.

At the appointed hour, we all crammed into the TV room with paper-plated hamburgers and hot dogs. Sweet tea and lemonade sloshed in red plastic cups. I cranked up the TV's volume to let the drama commence at this once-a-year contest.

As usual, forty thousand yellow hot dog hat–wearing spectators amassed in front of the stage while millions across the world amassed in front of their TVs. The essence of roasting hot dogs wafted through our den as if we were part of the Coney Island crowd.

The straw hat danced on the silver-tongued emcee's head as he whipped the throng into a fever. Nervous competitors on stage watched as the crowd erupted as reigning champ Joey snaked his way through the horde riding a mustard-colored chariot perched on the shoulders of four strong men.

My heart quickened as Chestnut dismounted and climbed the stage to join his fellow eaters. He ceremoniously assumed his position at the center of the long and laden banquet table. Plates of neatly stacked franks and buns awaited each contender alongside plastic tubs of water.

Endorphins flooded my body as the emcee counted down. *Can Joey possibly eat seventy-two?* "Five, four, three, two, one . . . go!"

Frenzied fist-to-mouth jamming commenced. Every competitor has his or her own style. Joey's well-oiled method is to soak two buns in water, smash them into a ball in his fist, cram them into his mouth, and . . . GULP. Then he noshes two dogs at a time as he shoves them in, his front teeth like a buzz saw, his cheeks protruding chipmunk-style and . . . GULP. Repeat. Repeat. Minimum mastication required. He rocks his body up and down, harnessing gravity in an amazing display of skill, concentration, and execution.

The act is not pretty, but it is beautiful. It is not a "tasting" for ye of the dainty palate. It is not nibbling or tinkering. It is a major league speed feed. A face-stuffing vortex. A food orgy fit for the ancient Romans.

Joey set out methodically and rapidly. Early on, he leapt ahead of the competition. Most were not remotely close to the champ's world-class abilities and were immediately exposed as pretenders.

But Joey's winning or losing was irrelevant to my bet— I needed 72 HDB to win, a 7.2 per minute pace. My eyes oscillated between Jaws, the clock, his current total, and the graphic displaying the current per-minute pace. Halfway through, he had noshed at a torrid and merciless pace, one not likely sustainable. I worried he had gorged *too* fast, for fear he'd need the bucket beside his feet and would suffer the resulting disqualification.

Toward the finale, I stood and started counting aloud as Joey continued noshing like a locomotive. *Forty-one, forty-two.* My palms grew moist. *Fifty-five, fifty-six.* "Shake and bake, baby!" My knuckles turned white on my balled fists, my heart pounded like NASCAR pistons. I fist-pumped with every dog. *Sixty-seven, sixty-eight.* Only seconds remained. *Sixty-nine, seventy.* My hands shot up. He gulped two more buns and the last two franks were on their way. Quick, time is r-u-n-n-i-n-g o-u-t. YES. *Seventy-one* and *seventy-two* were in his mouth and he gulped as the bell tolled.

YES. *Ha, ha, ha.* "Yeah, baby. Every*body*!" Hugs and high-fives all around our TV room. Mustard-colored confetti spewed the on-stage contestants.

One commentator called it "the greatest achievement in the history of man." Scholars can debate that issue ad nauseam, but surely Joey's triumph must be in the conversation for greatest achievement, at least in the top three, and easily the biggest story of 2017.

As you can see, if the Kentucky Derby is the most exciting two minutes in sports, Nathan's Hot Dog Eating Contest is the most exciting ten minutes.

Joey's 72 HDB totaled twenty thousand calories. During the TV interview immediately following the contest, Joey stood triumphant with one hand resting atop the trophy, the metallic Mustard Belt draped over his shoulder. He grinned and said, "I feel good." (Don't you know his breath smelled minty fresh?) For obvious reasons, I doubted that statement.

Shortly afterward, Socrates telephoned. "Shit is about to shoot out of Jaws's ass like a whistle. He could shit through the eye of a needle at thirty paces."

"No way," I said. "Maybe through a tractor tire, but not the eye of a needle." Makes me wonder about the time he set the world record for jalapeño poppers by downing 118 in ten minutes. Probably needed an assistant to douse his arse with a fire extinguisher that night.

So, the world anxiously awaits next July Fourth to see if Joey "Jaws" Chestnut can win his eleventh World Championship. How long can he hold the crown? Will anyone ever dominate again like Jaws? Who will emerge as the new King of the Hill? How high can they go?

After today's performance, I'm here to tell you, my friends, that Joey Chestnut, chomp champ, the best eater in history, is the Greatest Athlete of Our Time.

(Note to self: Consider turning pro. Rise above your fellow Walmart shoppers, those legions of amateur competitive eaters. Go forth and fill your buggy with great quantities of hot dogs, Ice Cream Sandwiches, and jalapeño poppers. Better snag a fire extinguisher, too.)

2018 POSTSCRIPT—SNATCHING VICTORY FROM THE JAWS OF DEFEAT

Joey was gunning for his eleventh world title at Nathan's. Vegas set the over/under at 72.5 HDB, even higher than Joey's miraculous 72 the year prior. Again, a crazy high number, but still I bet the OVER.

Megatoad came out fast and wrenched an early lead. Joey set into a "vicious rhythm" (his words afterward), and with the esophagus of a champion, overtook the Toad around the three-minute mark. He gradually built an insurmountable lead, the only question being whether he could best last year's seventy-two.

Even though Joey set a blistering pace, when the contest ended, they declared his winning total to be sixty-four. That low number felt odd because Joey had gobbled with great speed throughout. Even worse, I had lost my OVER bet. Cursing under my breath, I turned off the TV and moved on. Later that evening, the news reported a mistake. Joey had actually pounded 74 HDB, not 64! The contest counters, who deserve a good flogging, somehow and inexcusably missed a plate of ten.

Joey set yet another world record and is World Champion for the eleventh time, placing him in the company of golfer Walter Hagen (eleven majors) and Bill Russell (eleven NBA titles).

Better yet, I won the OVER bet after all. *Yeah, baby.*

GLIMPSE INTO THE FUTURE

What type of human is capable, in a significant way, of topping seventy-four hot dogs and buns in ten minutes? I can't envision it unless we start engineering the body for the sport.

We could tinker with genetics over a period of generations. Science tells us that our DNA mutates, adapts, and evolves based on external influences. If we, say, mandate competitive eating in grades K–12, we would gradually develop larger mouths, jaws, gullets, and stomachs.

Or, being the impatient species that we are, we could

surgically engineer champions with prosthetic parts, à la Dr. Frankenstein. Elastic lips, and jaws that unhinge like a snake's. PVC pipe for a gullet. Cast-iron pot for a stomach. Anything to win, right?

Our eating machine sporting a grotesque face like a large-mouth bass will roam cocktail parties scarfing all the hors d'oeuvres before heading to the kitchen.

Brace yourself, my friends. Future humankind will be a product of current times, and the hallmark of current times is gluttony.

CINCO DE TSUNAMI

One school of thought contends that a tequila high is superior to those of other alcoholic beverages, that it makes us crazy. Many people, including me, subscribe to that theory of superiority even though the scientific community begs to differ.

Based on my own research and empirical evidence gathering, I theorize that the tequila-producing Mexican blue agave plant harbors ancient mystical powers. It should be on the list of "psychoactive" plants along with peyote, coca, and poppy, but I'm happy it's not, because it's readily available at any liquor store.

Scientists claim that studies show any and all types of alcoholic drinks have the same effect on the human body—we convert the alcohol into ethanol, and . . . ethanol is ethanol. Ergo, they claim tequila makes us no loopier than do other liquors.

(Probably tee-totaling scientists who, like most academicians, have no actual hard experience in the field in which they preach. A glass of chardonnay with your colleagues at a reception to celebrate another PhD does not qualify as deep tequila-drinking research.)

How, then, would those scientists explain my most recent tequila escapade?

At a backyard Cinco de Mayo party, I congenially

joined some friends and we proceeded to quaff pitchers of margaritas. Our hostess, Sheila, sauntered out with a fresh bottle of tequila in one hand while balancing a tray of shot glasses, salt, and lime slices on the other.

Two virile college kids began rapidly knocking back shots, and I, in my manned-up, high noon at the O.K. Corral bravado, tried to hang with the young bucks shooter for shooter.

The last thing I remember is Tequila Sheila giggling as she leaned over to refill my glass. That last snort hit me like a tsunami.

I am a tourist convalescing from surgery, lounging in a chair on the beach of some small, coastal Oregon town. I gingerly raise my foot with its newly inserted pins and screws and ease it onto an adjoining chair. A large sock covers the cast, failing in its mission to block the sand.

Suddenly, the ground trembles. At first, it's as if a semi-truck is rumbling by. Then the terrain starts undulating like the rolling sea. I crash to the ground and there is nothing to grab to stabilize me. I hold my busted foot in the air, my mind gripped in shock.

In the Cascadia subduction zone, shifting of tectonic plates at the fault line just thirty miles offshore has caused an underwater quake. Natives know to run for the nearby hills when the sea starts roiling.

"You've got fifteen minutes to make it to higher ground or you'll be swamped," claimed a blog I read when researching the town.

Sirens are blaring and everybody hightails it inland like

roaches running from a fire. I know I'll never make it on my own with my bad foot. No one comes to help. I'm stranded—I'm doomed.

My frantic eyes scan the ocean. Waves are curling toward the sky as a giant wall of water looms before me.

The first wave washes out the sand 'round my butt. The next one crashes over my head. The games begin.

I am lifted and slammed to the ground then lifted again, over and over, catapulting farther inland, crashing into buildings as flying and floating objects collide into me.

I'm battered, broken, and barely conscious when I suddenly switch direction as I'm swept out to sea, sucked deep underwater at breakneck speed, tumbling head over heels like a rag doll. I black out . . .

That is when I lost vertical and crashed into Sheila's pink rhododendrons. Copious quantities of regurgitated matter hurled out of my mouth and splattered her prize-winning blossoms in which I floundered. The college boys righted my ship. My equilibrium askew, the ground seemed to undulate. The universe twirled inside my head and I caught a glimpse of God Himself gazing down on me. He nodded and winked, then all turned black . . .

Mr. Scientist, Mr. "Ethanol Is Ethanol," there is not enough grant money in Washington, DC, to replicate that experience with mere shots of beer, wine, vodka, or bourbon.

I rest my case.

ULTIMATE QUESTION ANSWERED

Today, I'm in a particularly philosophical mood. Alone, relaxed, comfortable, caffeinated, brain firing on all cylinders. Soft instrumental music sets the tone. Time for thought experimentation. Time to contemplate the Ultimate Question: What is the meaning of life?

For answers, we must look beyond our mere day-to-day trivialities and survey the grander scheme, the big picture, the whole enchilada. We can search for answers in religion, philosophy, and/or science. Today, let's explore science.

Be mindful that this discussion is based upon current understandings and beliefs by our learned scientific community, the same group that once proclaimed Earth to be the center of the universe and that masturbation leads to blindness and insanity.

For starters, you must realize that our planet is but a tiny, tiny speck in the universe. Try to wrap your head around these numbers:

In our solar system, we have our star, the Sun, around which Earth orbits. Our Sun is just one of one hundred billion stars in our Milky Way galaxy. The Milky Way is but one of ten trillion galaxies in the "observable" universe. These galaxies house around three hundred sextillion stars (300,000,000,000,000,000,000,000). And each star, like ours, has its own planetary system.

(Disclaimer: The above numbers vary among experts, so they may be off by a sextillion or two, but I believe the big picture is evident.)

Three hundred sextillion stars, my friends, is a large number. And that's just all we can currently observe. The universe may be infinite; we are not sure. (As an aside, if it is infinite, there is probably an exact copy of you somewhere out there. Imagine that! On the other hand, if the universe is finite, I want to know what lies on the other side. Another universe? Maybe three hundred sextillion universes.)

So when I say Earth is a speck in the universe, I mean big-time inconsequential and infinitesimal. Therefore, when we contemplate the Ultimate Question, we need to understand that our role in the grand scheme is nothing. Trifling at best.

Yet here we are, inhabitants of a mass of magna-laden rock teetering in a delicate and improbable balance while spinning on its axis at 1,000 mph and hurtling in its orbit around the Sun at 67,000 mph. What can possibly go wrong? What if . . .

What if the Sun dies? You know every star dies, right? The Sun is a mass of flaming matter that is in the process of burning out. Scientists *estimate* that we have a few billion years left. What if they are wrong again? They say when the Sun starts dying, it will first expand and move closer to Earth. At first, the oceans will boil, then evaporate, then the planet will be vaporized. Mankind will be toast, figuratively and literally.

Suppose a black hole floats into our solar system and swallows Earth? Earth will be sucked into the vortex and torn asunder. The black hole will swallow the Sun, too, as it joins the residue of its former planets in a mass of roaring, superheated dust and gas. Our solar system will be transformed into a circular inferno of dead inhabitants it once housed. We will be annihilated—pulverized and liquidated.

What if something knocks Earth off its solar orbit? What could cause this? An asteroid could smack us, much like the ten-kilometer asteroid that wiped out the dinosaurs 65 million years ago. That "Extinction Event," by the way, was the most recent of *five*, count five, such extinction events in the last 540 million years.

The asteroid's collision with Earth will choke the skies with debris, starving Earth of the Sun's energy, throwing a wrench in photosynthesis and causing destruction up and down the food chain. But if any of us survive, the asteroid will knock Earth off course, altering temperatures, and survivors will either fry or freeze. Mankind will be kaput.

Perhaps Earth will have a geological upheaval causing a massive bout of volcanoes, which some scientists believe was the cause of the dinosaur extinction. What if Earth's molten core cools, or we get slammed with a gamma ray burst or solar storms, or the universe goes to pieces in its final "Big Rip"? Mankind will be wiped out and each one of us simultaneously called to our eternal rest.

What about the *ongoing* mass extinction caused by human activity, what some say will be the "Sixth Extinction," caused by global warming, pandemic disease, maybe an engineered disease, nuclear war, artificial intelligence, robot ascension, and/or overpopulation? *Adios, amigos. Hasta la vista.*

Think I am being hyperbolic? The late Stephen Hawking, the famed theoretical physicist, wouldn't have thought so. He predicted that humankind has about a hundred years to find a new planet. (He later increased his drop-dead estimate to six hundred years.) He cited the alchemy of global warming, overdue asteroid strikes, epidemics, and population growth.

In light of these weighty considerations, I've arrived at my personal answer to the Ultimate Question—the meaning of life—at least based upon beliefs of our brethren in the scientific community, boiled down to one logical conclusion: *We're screwed.*

Fortuna, goddess of fortune and luck, may boink us at any moment.

Extinction events notwithstanding, life, my friends, is a fatal condition. You'll not get out alive.

Now that you are cognizant of these realities, haveth no fear; that's why God gave us beer. And when the moon ascends to the astrological eighth house—that of death—and simply hunkering down in your recliner is risky, time for whiskey.

OLYMPIC REBOOT

Do you ever find certain Olympic events—summer and winter—a bit boring? I have ideas to overhaul the entire Games, to jazz things up, to inject some real modern-day spice. With so many electronic devices chockablock with media competing for our attention these days, the Olympics must be extra special to maintain their popularity and ratings (low ratings equals no sponsors equals no teams) to thus ensure their viability and continued existence. These new Olympics will put reality TV to shame.

Due to space constraints, I will synopsize a few of my proposals so you can get a flavor. Rulebooks for each sport will require a Herculean revamp.

First off, there needs to be a new, overarching rule for all Olympic races—foot races, cycling, swimming, skiing, skating, snowboarding, and others. The rule emanates from the Right Honorable sport of Roller Derby. In it, as two teams skate 'round and 'round the track, rules allow for blockers to lower their shoulder and lay the boom on their opponents, sending them flying ass over teakettle as the jammer zips past to score.

For all Olympic races, expanded rules will allow pushing, grabbing, elbowing, punching, body blocking, tripping, even poking the eye Three Stooges style. Competitors may use only equipment currently allowed for that sport. For instance, if your sport allows ski poles, they will serve as marvelous tools to trip, push, slap, or jab an opponent. No guns, knives, billy clubs, and the like allowed. "Anything goes" will be the new mantra for races. Time to flip our athletes from buttercups back to gladiators.

There will be no more individually timed events such as downhill skiing, bobsleigh, and luge. No more individually performed events such as shot put, pole vault, ice skating, and pommel horse. There must be at least three competitors or teams on the course, court, or floor for each event.

Imagine the excitement! In downhill skiing with six competitors shooting out of the gate at 80 mph, just a wee push from your ski pole will send an opponent head over heels in spectacular fashion. In the 100-meter sprint, tripping anyone ahead of you will become an art. Bobsleigh will combine bumper cars with stock-car racing, sans the deafening roar of engines. Snowboard cross will be a midair boxing match.

Ski jumping will be a hoot. Trip your neighbor at the start and watch him slide facedown the length of the hill then launch like a sack of potatoes. Better yet, whack your neighbor's legs on takeoff, sending him pinwheeling, flipping, and spiraling. Those landings would be fantastical.

A universal rule change: dump the metric system and use the good ole US standard system. Between you and me, no one actually knows the metric system anyway. The beauty of the US system, unlike metric, is that the units of measure have no predictable relationship to one another. One must think harder to use the US system, which in turn keeps the brain sharp. Must stave off Alzheimer's, you know.

Now for a few more rules:

HIGH PLATFORM DIVING

Time to rethink this sport. In current diving standards, the less splash, the better. You're looking for a *non-event*. How boring.

Wouldn't it be more entertaining to watch a new Olympic event, "The High Platform Can Opener"? None of that twisting and flipping and technical shit. Just two judging criteria: how high and how spectacular the splash.

I initially conceived the High Platform Cannon Ball, but I've always produced higher splashes with that other backyard classic, the Can Opener. Given the height of that platform, I bet my Can Opener could splash the spectators in the cheap seats and plop official Olympic pool water right into their official Olympic souvenir beer cups.

It would take talent to enter the water at a perfect thirty-five-degree angle, one leg straight as a board, toes pointed, the other leg tucked tight against your chest. The backsplash could rip your face off. No masks allowed!

Time to let us big-boned people in on the diving fun. I think I could check "Olympic Gold Medal" off my bucket list.

As I watch platform diving, it makes my stomach flip when the diver's head nearly collides with the platform as they launch into their routine. I *like* that style of drama.

Wouldn't it be a hoot and headline news if a diver whacked his head on the platform but kept somersaulting as planned, spewing a red spray of blood all the way down like water off a pinwheel?

Maybe turn *that* into an event.

"Tonight, we have the finals of the women's High Platform Whack-Your-Head Dive. As you probably know, the rules award bonus points if the diver is unconscious when she hits the water. This will be REALLY EXCITING."

CURLING

Each team will have a hypersensitive IED bomb embedded into one, and only one, stone. Nobody will know which stone until it whacks into another—*BOOM*. Russian Roulette Curling. The excitement and anticipation will be breathtaking, not knowing which stone. Bet that would keep those annoying sweepers at bay.

SWIMMING

After converting the pool to saltwater, a (hungry) great white shark will prowl the pool. Bet the old records will quickly succumb.

TRACK AND FIELD RELAY

The hair-trigger dynamite baton will explode on impact. Bet you'll see a lot fewer baton drops.

EQUESTRIAN JUMPING

Remember, there must be at least three competitors on the course at one time. Wouldn't it be a blast to watch a rider ram his riding crop up the ass of his competitor's horse just prior to launch?

There you go. Just a few examples. I can overhaul the entire Games and bring them into the twenty-first century.

As for roller derby, isn't it time we made *it* an Olympic sport?

FAST TIMES IN THE VOMITORY

This is an edited version of my true story published in Modern Drunkard Magazine, *August 2005, under the pseudonym "P. W. Lewis."*

The torso of my troubled body dangled from my eighth-floor dormitory window. As I puked and gagged, my trainers gripping my belt to prevent my tumble, I realized that it's not an easy feat to outdrink a seven-foot Indian Chief.

The dorm's updraft spread and floated vomit like a parachute in its plunge to the building's rather spartan front entrance eighty feet below. The first volley sprayed and splattered unsuspecting chumps standing in the landing zone. Dribble oozed down the brick wall beneath the sill.

Thus ended my match with Big Chief Ed, a dead ringer for the giant Indian who played the ersatz deaf-mute in *One Flew Over the Cuckoo's Nest*. This brave didn't waste words either.

Big Chief lived next door in my dorm. When I arrived on campus, this Brooklyn boy with aspirations to become a cop introduced me to Shanahan's on the Square, his favorite downtown pub. He personally oversaw the engraving of my initials on a pewter mug. My chalice hung on a pegboard among dozens more. Ed would suck down his lager then wave his vessel while singing "When Irish Eyes Are Smiling," crying like a girl at Christmas. Come to find out, an Irishman had wrangled his way into Chief's tribe and it apparently meant the world to him.

The big guy and I were pals, on equal footing, no grudges, no debts, until one infamous evening. I was in my room studying when the giant burst in, slammed the door, and braced his humongous 350-pound body against it.

He detonated the mother of all farts, copious even for a beer-bellied, pizza-eating machine. The temperature must have skyrocketed ten degrees. My face flushed, eyes watered, and barf fought its way up my gullet. I desperately tried to wrestle my way around him and out the door. Not a chance. He stonewalled me cold.

I bolted across the room to open the window, but he caught me and pinned me to the bed, laughing like a fucking hyena. Degenerates standing outside hooted and hollered. It was the low point of my college matriculation. My new life mission? Revenge!

One evening at Shanahan's, Chief marched in and announced that he could outdrink anybody there. Just so happens I made a similar boast in jest earlier that day. Being trapped by my bravado and challenged by Goliath right there in the open, in front of my loyal associates, left me with no viable choice but to defend my manhood.

I cracked a twisted grin. "Okay, okay, but not tonight. I'm already too far down the road. Besides, we need time to iron out details."

Big Chief's lazy smile faded and his steely brown eyes

stared down my blinking blues. "Any time . . . any place."
I hadn't seen that look. My scalp tingled.

"Well then, by God," I said, "you're gonna have to
knock back a six-pack head start."

"Bullshit," he said. "Are you a man or a fucking Girl
Scout?"

Thus began negotiations. We set the match for Friday
night two weeks out to allow for rules, strategies, training,
handicapping, and bets. Central to the wagering was the
deal between us two combatants: "Loser pays for the beer
and no head start," he insisted. We split the difference—
he would down three beers just before the waving of the
green flag.

Side bets soared pegging Chief a 2-to-1 favorite—low
odds considering the bastard weighed twice as much as
me. Some comrades had witnessed my game, though, and
I was proud they considered me a mere 2-to-1 underdog.

Friday fight night shaped up to mark yet another
monotonous weekend at this staid SEC college where frat
boys headed to adventurous destinations, leaving us poor
saps and foreign-exchange students to fend for ourselves.

But something special was brewing in Room 808, North
Tower—we were preparing to burn down the house.
Overseers were icing two cases of beer as my roommate,
SnakeEye, and I headed out for my pre-match meal.

A student of modest means, SnakeEye donned his
signature Che Guevara beret and oversized green army
jacket. As he often did, he lined his jacket pockets with
aluminum foil then steered us to an all-you-can-eat buffet

so he could stuff his pockets with food. (I had to smell that damn food for a week as he reheated it bit by bit. But I digress.)

On advice of Kick, a senior living down the hall who spent time in rehab and thus a drinking guru, I Roman-orgy feasted on all things fried. "Grease will make beer slide through you like shit through a goose," Kick waxed eloquent. It made sense at the time.

We negotiated the drinking pit to be my room. "Home court advantage is huge," I explained to my team. "My bed, my music, my shit. My back will literally be against the wall in my own space. No place to retreat. I must defend, dammit to hell."

For my competition robe, Kick borrowed a purple silk number from the Chinese exchange student down the hall. I wore "Ole Lucky," my granddad's John Deere cap. We cranked up an Allman Brothers album on SnakeEye's turntable and lit incense. My trainers took turns giving me neck and shoulder rubs.

Suddenly, the theme from *Rocky* blared in the hallway and I was sure the chancellor's wife's teacups were rattling. I plugged my ears and stared in wonder as Big Chief and his entourage of thugs strutted in carrying a boombox the size of your average midget.

Chief wore his special Washington Redskins polyester shorts, the ones he never washed. His bare feet revealed long, gnarly toes that could strangle a grown man, and he knew they repulsed me. I was gob-smacked by two black hash marks smeared on each cheek—war paint!

The referee, whose main job was to prevent cheating, forced the thug to turn off his boombox—home court rules. Chief plopped down on SnakeEye's pillow and flexed his butt cheeks, seemingly working half the pillow up his ass. Gawking spectators and fellow bottle-suckers took their places.

We watched and trash-talked as the big son of a bitch leisurely drank his first three beers, his mandatory head start. He went to piss, remounted SnakeEye's pillow, scratched his nuts, belched, nodded, and said, "Let the games begin."

Kick, reminding me of our brilliant strategy, winked and said, "Drink like hell." Big Chief had a different game plan. When the bell clanged, it was as if lightning struck his elbow and he guzzled four beers by the time I'd finished my first.

Sticking to my plan, I drank like hell, steady and fast, while Chief paced me in lockstep. The scorekeeper kept shouting, "Three up. Three up. Three up."

I attempted trickery—knocking back two while he was pissing, but he fired right back at me. I tried slow. I tried fast. "Three up," echoed the refrain.

After consultation with my team, I reached into my suitcase for Jack Daniels. "A toast to the Irish, by God." The big bastard's eyes grew moist. "Bring it on," he barked.

Chief didn't even wipe his mouth after whiskey snorts. He slammed the empty shot glass on the tabletop and stared me down.

"Three up. Three up. Three up."

I leapt for the scorekeeper and choked his throat. "Say that one more time and I'm throwing your ass out the window."

Best I could focus after four whiskey shots, I studied Chief's face to see how much game he had left. He sat stoic, legs crossed Indian style, looking bored. My squint bounced from cold, dark eyes to war paint and back. It was evident the cocksucker had a hollow leg and I couldn't beat him fair and square.

"Hey," I slurred, "what's say we put a towel under the door and smoke some reefer?"

"No way," he said. "Remember, I'm gonna be a fuckin' cop!"

"Psst," I whispered in his ear, pointing to my hand. "Let's take these *little red pills.* We'll feel very, very great." I intended to conceal mine under my tongue until I could spit them out, à la Jack Nicholson in the aforementioned *One Flew Over the Cuckoo's Nest.*

He waved me off with the back of his hand. "Get outta here."

My added stamina garnered from training runs on the trail skirting campus was fading fast. On advice of Kick, my sham advisor, and woefully too late to make a difference, I took some calisthenics. "It'll sober you up," he shouted. In retrospect, I think it accelerated my demise.

About the time the Chinese exchange student started dancing, the change washed over me. Sadly for SnakeEye, the first heavy spew sailed in a direct hit to his turntable.

"Oh my," I mumbled. *Someone forgot to close the lid.* This

was the same turntable SnakeEye wouldn't let me touch for months after I moved in, afraid I'd somehow fuck it up. He owned scant few possessions, and that record player and his albums were the jewels of his very existence.

An imminent surge of puke gurgled up my throat and burned my nostrils. I lunged for the open window and luckily snagged on the sill, dizzied by depths below. Hands grabbed my belt and I hung there, spewing, gagging, and trying to catch my breath.

Fresh trouble erupted from behind. "You son of a bitch!" SnakeEye screamed as he went berserk over his precious turntable. He attempted to overpower my trainers and shove me out the window. Fortunately for me, Big Chief pounced on SnakeEye and handily restrained him.

Somebody yelled from far below, "Hey, Ralph!" Then another, "Ralph." *Great.* A taunting crowd was soon chanting in cadence, "Go, Ralph. Go, Ralph. Go, Ralph."

You bastards, I thought. But for the grace of God, your ass would be up here heaving your guts. Your time will come, you swine.

By now, my whole team was cursing me for losing. Having taken the odds, each had just blown a week's meal money and all were stewing in foul humor. Ass over teakettle, my rear end aimed straight for their faces. I knew when I started sharting my pants and this became an interactive sport, my trainers would instinctively release their grip on my belt.

I had enough wits about me to right myself, and that's when I projectile-hurled onto the purple silk bathrobe. The

Chinese student summarily stopped dancing. Party over. I stumbled down the hall to the bathroom and shower. Big Chief whooped me good.

Legend has it that he and his tribe of thugs went drinking at Shanahan's later that night, but I can't swear to it.

The evening was not a total loss. My dribble, drool, and DNA waterfall etched the brick below our window, creating a stained monument to the occasion, earning me a certain amount of bankable notoriety and swag on campus.

Our drinking match became a romantic tale of heroism around Shanahan's, backed up with a pay-to-play field trip. Gazing at the window on high from the asphalt parking lot, I'd boast like a circus barker and we'd toast the mosaic nick in the brick.

Training for the rematch began immediately. I have kept at it for thirty years—long after the chances for said contest on this Earth ended. Big Chief Ed achieved his dream of becoming a cop, but sadly, an outlaw's bullet smote him from this life.

We shall have our rematch in heaven. Until then, my friend, may Irish eyes smile upon you . . . but when that day comes, you're going down.

ACKNOWLEDGMENTS

Writing a book is a team sport, and I owe thanks to numerous people.

Many folks unwittingly contributed to this effort. I could list them all, but I dare not.

Three that I will salute, each an endless fountain of comic relief, are Lawton Tollison, Dr. Lee Bell, and my brother, Bruce Gregg. Keep 'em coming, boys.

Many thanks to the team at Mountain Arbor Press.

My deepest gratitude to my wife, Maureen, who *wittingly* contributed in so many ways. She is fodder in a few stories, but she knows that I wouldn't satirize and parody her if I didn't love her, for there is no sound more beautiful than her laughter, no sight more pleasing than her smile, and no gifts more valuable than her love . . . and her sea of red-ink edits. She is a proper lady, so please know that she held her nose while editing some entries in this book.

Captain Molly says,
"May you have fair winds and following seas."

ABOUT THE AUTHOR

Jameson Gregg won 2015 Georgia Author of the Year for his debut book, *Luck Be A Chicken: a comic novel*. His works appear in literary anthologies, magazines, and newspapers, and he has won numerous other humor genre awards.

Jameson practiced law for twenty years in Georgia's Golden Isles and achieved the highest national ranking for lawyers before hanging up his wingtips to pursue his passion for writing. Offbeat college jobs influencing his worldview include Mississippi River tugboat deckhand, taxi driver, iceman in a chicken plant, and traveling circus promoter (trapeze artist he is not!).

A Mississippi native and graduate of Ole Miss and Mississippi College School of Law, he resides in the mountains of Georgia with his wife, Maureen.

Visit his website at www.jamesongregg.com.

Other Books
by Jameson Gregg

Luck Be A Chicken: a comic novel